T0280132

Best Easy Day Hikes
Great Smoky Mountains National Park

Help Us Keep This Guide Up to Date

Every effort has been made by the author and editors to make this guide as accurate and useful as possible. However, many things can change after a guide is published—regulations change, facilities come under new management, and so forth.

We would love to hear from you concerning your experiences with this guide and how you feel it could be improved and kept up to date. While we may not be able to respond to all comments and suggestions, we'll take them to heart, and we'll also make certain to share them with the author. Please send your comments and suggestions to falconeditorial @rowman.com.

Thanks for your input!

Best Easy Day Hikes Series

Best Easy Day Hikes Great Smoky Mountains National Park

Third Edition

Randy Johnson

ESSEX, CONNECTICUT

FALCONGUIDES®

An imprint of Globe Pequot, the trade division of
The Rowman & Littlefield Publishing Group, Inc.
4501 Forbes Blvd., Ste. 200
Lanham, MD 20706
www.rowman.com

Falcon and FalconGuides are registered trademarks and Make Adventure Your Story is a trademark of The Rowman & Littlefield Publishing Group, Inc.

Distributed by NATIONAL BOOK NETWORK

British Library Cataloguing-in-Publication Information Available

Library of Congress Cataloging-in-Publication Data

Names: Johnson, Randy, 1951– author.
Title: Best easy day hikes Great Smoky Mountains National Park / Randy
    Johnson.
Description: Third edition. | Essex, Connecticut : FalconGuides, [2024] |
    Series: Best easy day hikes series | "A previous edition of this book
    was published by FalconGuides in 2010"—Copyright page.
Identifiers: LCCN 2023056282 (print) | LCCN 2023056283 (ebook) | ISBN
    9781493076598 (paper : acid-free paper) | ISBN 9781493076604
    (electronic)
Subjects: LCSH: Day hiking—Great Smoky Mountains National Park (N.C. and
    Tenn.)—Guidebooks. | Hiking—Great Smoky Mountains National Park (N.C.
    and Tenn.)—Guidebooks. | Walking—Great Smoky Mountains National Park
    (N.C. and Tenn.)—Guidebooks. | Trails—Great Smoky Mountains National
    Park (N.C. and Tenn.)—Guidebooks. | Great Smoky Mountains National Park
    (N.C. and Tenn.)—Guidebooks.
Classification: LCC GV199.42.G73 J64 2024 (print) | LCC GV199.42.G73
    (ebook) | DDC 796.5109768/89—dc23/eng/20231227
LC record available at https://lccn.loc.gov/2023056282
LC ebook record available at https://lccn.loc.gov/2023056283

Contents

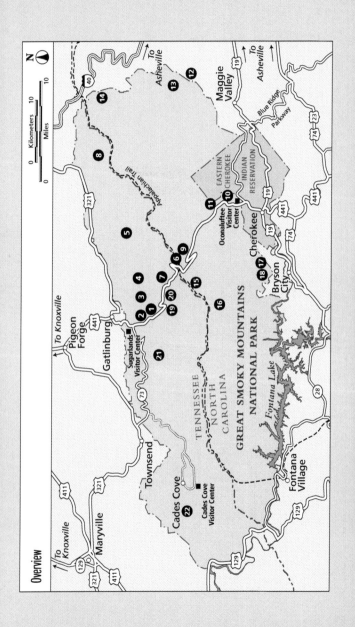

Introduction

Great Smoky Mountains is the country's most popular national park. That distinction is due to much more than just proximity to nearby urban areas. This United Nations–designated International Biosphere Reserve—one of the most diverse ecosystems on Earth—is a temperate rainforest that's world-class lush. Despite extensive logging in the early 1900s, parts of the park escaped the logger's saw, so tracts of old-growth timber remain. The 800 square miles of the Smokies is one of the largest intact natural areas in the eastern United States. The Smokies contain entire watersheds of peaks and valleys completely devoid of trails. Though motorists rarely see it, hikers on park paths can savor that inspiring wilderness on even short walks.

Ecosystems and Weather

A huge area of the park soars above 4,500 feet to more than 6,600 feet, where cool summers and deep-snow winters prevail in the spruce-fir ecosystem of the Canadian forest zone (comprising red spruce and Fraser fir). Vast portions of the park also sprawl below 2,500 feet, where a diverse pine and oak forest reigns and summer can bring sticky, even hot weather. Between these two ecosystems, elevation and aspect (the location of the land in damp valley or on dry ridge, on the sunny side or in the shade) yield woodlands of three general types. Luxuriant hemlock forests, now being decimated by the invasive hemlock woolly adelgid, once flourished up to about 4,000 feet. Hardwoods soar from the mid-elevations to the summit spruce-fir zone. The damp, deep-soil valleys of the cove hardwood forests contain the park's tallest trees, often yellow poplar. Higher, above 4,500 feet, northern hardwoods of beech and birch intersperse among evergreens.

The Smokies' location and range of elevation bestow a uniquely northern climate. The best wildflower walks are invariably during April (with May a close second), as warm weather returns—especially lower in the park. Higher up, spring often hasn't sprung till very late May or early June. June, July, and August bring the warmest weather, but late August starts the temperature dip to autumn at lofty locations. By late September, autumn color is evident, and it's everywhere by mid- to late October.

Spring and summer are the Smokies' rainy season. There are beautiful days, but be prepared for misty rains, thunderstorms, and yes, even torrential downpours. Rainfall ranges between 55 and 85 inches annually, from low to high elevation—so rain gear should be in everyone's day pack. Fall generally dries out nicely—and quickly leads to winter.

The "Top of Old Smoky" is one long, very high ridge that often influences the weather. From late October, and especially November through March and even into April, snow can be light and atmospheric (early and late) or drifted to awe-inspiring depths that close the Newfound Gap Road between Cherokee, North Carolina, and Gatlinburg, Tennessee. Spring and fall hikers should be prepared: Bring a hat, light gloves, and warm fleece garments to layer under waterproof outerwear should the wind whip and the temps dip. Winter hikers and especially campers bound for the highest summits should know the weather in advance (visit the park's website), bring ample, energy-filled foods, sophisticated winter gear, and the expert knowledge of how to use it.

History

The Smokies is the perfect place to take a history hike. Evidence of times past is everywhere—especially along trails from late fall to spring, when retreating vegetation reveals walls, steps, foundations, and decaying structures.

Native American lore and legends wrap like the mists around these mountains, the once-idyllic realm of the Cherokee. Ironically, six years before Andrew Jackson banished the Smokies' Cherokees to their tragic Trail of Tears, a forced removal to Oklahoma in 1838, Hudson River School–era portrait artist George Catlin had proposed the concept of a "Nation's park" to protect "Indian civilization, wildlife, and wilderness" from destruction. Catlin's 1832 Indian portraits are among the classic images of the Old West. The proud Cherokee past stands out at various attractions just outside the park in the Cherokee Indians' Qualla Boundary reservation. The Oconaluftee River Trail near Cherokee is an introduction.

The arrival of later settlers is reflected in dozens of places, at sites where interpretive programs describe the lives of those whose early cabins, farms, mills, and, later, clapboard churches and houses still remain. In further irony, those residents also left the Smokies—but were compensated for their property—when state land purchases led to the National Park Service creating parks in the East. In Virginia's Shenandoah National Park, then the Great Smokies in North Carolina and Tennessee, and again along the Blue Ridge Parkway in North Carolina and Virginia, federal government programs eventually displaced residents from once private land. Earlier parks in the West were created on public land to begin with.

The Smokies is one of the nation's premier places to savor the iconic, early settler style of structure called the log cabin. To get the most out of the park, pick up the booklet *Log Cabins of the Smokies* when you stop at one of the park's visitor centers, or get one online at the Great Smoky Mountains Association (www.smokiesinformation.org). Other booklets feature the park's gristmills and churches.

Citizen Support of the Smokies

The Great Smoky Mountains Association (www.smokies information.org) and the Friends of the Smokies (www .friendsofthesmokies.org) are quintessential examples of the great work being done all over the nation by citizen groups that are raising money to bolster the shrinking budgets of individual parks. Some of these park support groups have special license plate programs (the "Friends" offer plates in both North Carolina and Tennessee) that dedicate the "vanity" fee to park programs. As befits our most visited national park, the two groups listed above are largely responsible for the insightful and inspiring interpretive efforts found all over the Smokies, including the trail brochures found at many paths. Indeed, the park's new Oconaluftee Visitor Center, dedicated in 2011, was funded entirely by these two organizations. Hikers in the park will also see ample evidence of the Friends of the Great Smokies' Trails Forever program, an effort that deploys a professional trail crew each summer to make impressive improvements to popular trails. Many trail entries in this book include recent Trails Forever maintenance activities. As the National Park Service celebrated its 100th anniversary in 2016, there's no doubt that the Smokies is one of the most effectively interpreted and protected parks in the nation, thanks to citizen support.

Please do your part. Besides buying a trail brochure and contributing at the donation boxes you'll see in the park, consider joining one of the above organizations. You won't need to hike more than a handful of trails in this book to become an enthusiastic supporter of the Smokies.

Park Regulations

Parking Fee Program

Every park visitor should understand Great Smoky Mountains National Park's mandatory parking sticker fee program.

Entry fees have been the norm at national parks since the beginning, but no entry fee was ever charged in the Smokies. That's because the park's main road, US 441, the Newfound Gap Road, is a public highway and major artery linking North Carolina and Tennessee.

That has long hobbled funding for what is now the most visited national park in the country. For years we've underfunded "America's best idea," our national parks, but in recent times, dedicated user fees have been implemented to focus added funds on busy parks where fees are collected. In 2023, a parking tag program called "Park It Forward" brought that kind of solution to the Smokies.

Anyone can stop at Newfound Gap and visit a restroom or point their smart phone at the view. But visitors and trail users who park for more than 15 minutes are required to display a modestly priced daily, weekly, or annual windshield/dashboard tag with the correct date and license plate.

For preplanned trips, all tags are easily purchased online at recreation.gov and either printed out at home or received by mail up to six months in advance. For spur of the moment visits, there are in-person sales sites during business hours at many visitor centers and businesses in and near the park, and for daily and weekly tags, automated, plentiful credit card tag machines are accessible 24 hours a day. All these options are described on the park's website under Plan Your Visit > Basic Information > Fees and Passes.

The tags are not location-specific (so hikers and especially backcountry campers should get to their trailheads early!). Nor are tags replaceable, refundable, transferable, or upgradable. The federal government's interagency pass, such as the senior pass that nets a discount on entrance and some other fees at national parks, does not replace the Smokies *parking* fee but does save money on the park's camping fees. But there are exemptions. For instance, no parking sticker is needed for motorists with a disabled parking placard or license plate who may want to pause in the park or sample one of the park's "Quiet Walkways" or very easy trails. And no parking tag is needed to park at a campsite rented in the park's car campgrounds.

Camping

The Great Smokies has ten frontcountry campgrounds accessible by car. They vary by elevation and offerings, with some sites available by advanced reservation and others on a first-come-first-serve basis (check the park's website for the latest details on season and reservations).

Since 2013, backcountry campers have been required to have advance reservations and a permit for all overnight camping in the park (a fee is charged). The Smokies is a very popular backpacking destination, so the park's regulations are extensive and policies differ for General Backcountry Permits and AT Thru-Hiker Permits. Visit the park's permit and reservation website for complete information and to process your permit (https://smokiespermits.nps.gov). Reservations can be made a month in advance of the first night of a trip itinerary. The park recommends calling the Backcountry Information Office as the preferred way to clarify camping regulations and ask trip-planning questions; open 8 a.m. to 5 p.m. daily, (865) 436-1297.

The brief regulations below are up to date at press time, but Smokies' hikers and campers should be sure to read the latest, most complete list of backcountry regulations on the park website. Violations can result in fines and jail time.

Camping is permitted only at designated campsites and shelters (no more than three consecutive nights at any backcountry campsite, and only one night per party is permitted at any shelter and at campsite 113). Maximum camping party size is eight (see website for special group restrictions). Fires are permitted only at designated sites in designated fire rings (create no new ones).

The Smokies is also home to the highest overnight accommodation in eastern America—LeConte Lodge, located atop Mount LeConte at 6,500 feet. Hiking to this full-service hostel is a ritual for many, and an experience akin to spending the night in one of the lofty backcountry lodges found in the European Alps or New Hampshire's White Mountains. For more on this option, see the hike description for the Alum Cave Trail (the "easy way" to Mount LeConte).

Dogs

Dogs are permitted in frontcountry campgrounds but must be leashed or enclosed at all times. They are prohibited on all trails, except a few, one featured in this book (the Oconaluftee River Trail, #10). Be sure to pick up after your pet.

Safety and Precautions

Animals

For fans of wildlife, the Smokies is a bonanza of observational opportunities. Deer, black bears, and other animals are seen often, and elk have been reintroduced (the latter often glimpsed near roads along the Newfound Gap Road and in Cataloochee Valley). The more rarely glimpsed wild hogs were introduced from Europe into North Carolina as game in the early twentieth century and still remain. Hikers who take less traveled trails and tread softly will encounter many wild park residents. That said, taking some precautions will keep your encounters on the safe side. Be sure to visit the park's website and review the wildlife viewing rules and regulations.

Be Bear Aware

Bears are a frequent sight in the Smokies. The park reminds visitors, especially hikers, that bears are wild animals and can behave unpredictably. If you encounter a bear (or any large animal for that matter) and are close enough to attract its attention or change its behavior, park regulations say you are too close. Never get closer than 150 feet. Back away slowly and attempt to get as far away as possible. If a bear becomes aggressive and follows you, do not run while you move off in a completely different direction. If the bear continues to approach, stand your ground, shout loudly, and act aggressively to scare the bear—use bear spray or even throw sticks and stones to run it off. You'll be more effective if you do this with a group of other hikers. If you are literally attacked, jettison your food and back out of the area. If you are being attacked and food is not the bear's objective, fight back in any way possible and with anything at hand.

In the backcountry, when not being carried or consumed, all food must be hung at least 10 feet off the ground to avoid tempting bears. Cables have been installed at campsites for this purpose. All human feces must be buried at least 6 inches, and all toilet use must take place at least 100 feet from campsites and water sources.

Snakes

The Smokies' venomous vipers include the timber rattler and the copperhead, both mostly at mid- to lower elevations. Luckily, of the twenty-thousand people a year who are bitten by poisonous snakes in the United States, only between six and fifteen die. The low death rate is due to several factors: Snake venom is relatively slow acting. Almost half of all snakebites do not include the injection of venom. And antivenin is widely available at hospitals.

The park's venomous snakes are generally heftier than harmless snakes and have triangular or arrow-shaped heads and vertically slit pupils (versus tube-shaped heads and round pupils for nonvenomous snakes). To avoid snakes, don't reach blindly behind logs and rocks, inspect wooded sites where you plan to sit, and watch where you step.

When to Go

Any hike in the park can be crowded if you go at the wrong time, so choose carefully. Best bets: Visit the park and hike lower-elevation trails during late fall, early winter, or early spring. In spring, summer, or fall, try to hike midweek or go as early in the morning as possible (especially with the Smokies' new parking tag program in place). A crowded parking lot will not affect you if you return to one after your hike!

In spring or fall, choose the time just before or after wildflowers bloom or foliage peaks—and go midweek! Ozone and other air pollutants have robbed the Smokies of its longest views, especially in summer. Consider visiting in winter, late fall, and early spring as—beyond encountering fewer people—the arrival of high-pressure weather systems tends to increase visibility. Also, fewer air pollution alerts can bestow health benefits on national park hikers, especially kids or people with breathing difficulties.

Bottom line: There's not much sense complaining about the crowds in the nation's most visited national park, especially if you come at a busy time. The Smokies is worth some vacation days. You will see fewer other folks if you choose less visited seasons and hike midweek.

Sampling the Smokies

Motoring

This guide includes trails all over the Smokies, so don't assume that the popular and at times crowded Newfound Gap Road trailheads are your only entrances to the park. Both sides of the Smokies offer adventurous motor tours that abut nice trails.

The Cataloochee Valley, on the southeast side of the park, leads to great streamside strolls past the preserved churches, homes, and schools of early settlers. The appeal here includes possible sightings of the elk that are being reintroduced. In the south, the Heintooga Spur Road branches from the Blue Ridge Parkway near Maggie Valley and passes the parkway's Balsam Mountain Campground and Picnic Area to form a loop that reaches the Oconaluftee Visitor Center via the Cherokee reservation's Big Cove Road.

From Gatlinburg, don't miss the Roaring Fork Motor Nature Trail. Buy the brochure at the trailhead, take the hikes along the route that are listed in this book, and enjoy the historic and scenic sites of one of the park's best motor tours. Also from Gatlinburg and the Sugarlands Visitor Center, the Little River and Laurel Creek Roads lead to Elkmont Campground and the park's Cades Cove area—the latter featuring a truly spectacular and extremely popular 11-mile, one-way loop (currently closed to cars Wednesday from May to September and open to pedestrians and bicyclists).

You'll also find access to these roads and Cades Cove from Townsend, Tennessee. Also near Townsend, the Rich Mountain Road and the recently reopened Parson Branch Road (built in 1838), both closed in winter, permit a visit to Cades Cove and exit via more lightly traveled roads through the heart of the park. Either or both of these roads are part of a big loop through and around the entire northwestern Smokies, using a portion of the Foothills Parkway. Visit the park's "Temporary Road and Facilities Closures" web page for vehicle restrictions and the latest on what's open. Better yet, sign up for the X (formerly Twitter) feed.

Shuttle Services

Hiker shuttles are available from companies just outside the park, so it's easy to start on one trail, hike out on another, and get a lift back to your car. Troll the Internet to find a shuttle service that meets your needs.

Surrounding Towns

The above road trips and shuttle options permit you to sample some of the Smokies' fascinating surrounding towns.

Cherokee

More than just another tourist town, Cherokee sits in the largest Indian reservation in eastern America. It is one of the premier destinations for parkway and Great Smokies visitors.

The Eastern Band of the Cherokee's stirring culture and history come alive in *Unto These Hills,* an outdoor drama that movingly tells the Trail of Tears saga (presented from early June to late August). The Museum of the Cherokee Indian has top-notch interactive exhibits. Oconaluftee Indian Village re-creates a Cherokee town with rich hands-on demonstrations. Crafts and fine arts created by members of the oldest Native American art organization are available at the Qualla Arts and Crafts Mutual, Inc. (http://visitcherokeenc.com).

The reservation is also home to Harrah's Cherokee, a major casino resort with diverse dining, upscale decor, and a new golf course. You must be over 21 to enter the casino, the only place in both Cherokee and on the reservation where beer, wine, and liquor are available (harrahscherokee.com).

Nearby attractions include the Great Smoky Mountains Railroad in Bryson City, 20 minutes from Cherokee (www.gsmr.com). Train excursions pass through Nantahala Gorge (one permits guests to raft their way back to town).

Also nearby is Nantahala Outdoor Center, which offers highly recommended rafting expeditions, an outfitter store, eateries, accommodations, and a great dose of southern Appalachian outdoor culture (www.noc.com).

Gatlinburg/Pigeon Forge

These are the towns Southerners think of when they conjure the term "mountain vacation." Gatlinburg's major attractions run the gamut from wax museums to Ripley's Believe It or Not (www.gatlinburg.com). This is an attractive, pedestrian-friendly village that—were it not for the aforementioned tourist attractions—would remind some of a European mountain village, where creeks and rivers rush through town in rock wall–enclosed gushers and condos cluster around the village core.

This is a ski town from December to March, so the European feel is furthered by the huge aerial tram you can take from town up to the slopes for summertime ice skating and to see the town's black bear and eagle habitats. Gatlinburg has the park's most diverse dining and watering holes (with liquor and Alcoholic Beverage Control Commission stores available). There are all kinds of chain hotels and cabins tucked into the woods, including some of the park's historic sites, which are reached through Gatlinburg on the Cherokee Orchard Road and Roaring Fork Motor Nature Trail.

Pigeon Forge is a glitzy strip of popular family attractions with comedy, music, and Christian religious shows as the main draws (www.pigeonforgechamber.com or www.mypigeonforge.com). There are fun, high-quality museums devoted to Elvis and dinosaurs, and there's even a Titanic replica "docked" to the strip. Dolly Parton's "Dollywood"— simply one of the best theme parks in the nation—leads the list of attractions at Pigeon Forge (www.dollywood.com). The fare runs to down-home and wholesome—chow down on a country-style fried chicken dinner at Miss Lillian's Smokehouse (named for Dolly's mother). The entertainment leans to pop and show tunes, but country, gospel, and mountain music are all appropriate to this southern Appalachian location, which gave us America's traditional music. You can watch the park's eagles and other birds of prey in a 30,000-square-foot aviary. And there's always the roller coasters—among the best in the country. The pool and health club at the modern Pigeon Forge Community Center are also open to the public.

But all this glitz is only icing on the real cake—Great Smoky Mountains National Park.

The 2016 Smokies Wildfires

In late November 2016, the largest known fire in the history of Great Smoky Mountains National Park erupted during exceptional drought conditions. Starting on the park's craggy peak called Chimney Tops, the Chimney Tops 2 Fire ultimately burned 11,410 acres in the park, just one of many wildfires that burned thousands of acres across western North Carolina, east Tennessee, and neighboring states during fall 2016. On November 28, high winds and dry conditions merged fires in the park and nearby Gatlinburg in Sevier County on the park's western border (which burned 6,494 acres). Rain and diminishing winds started reducing the fire on November 29, but full containment wasn't achieved until December 20. Ultimately, 14 people died and about 2,000 residential, commercial, and resort buildings, most in the vicinity of Gatlinburg, were destroyed or damaged. Nevertheless, the Tennessee Smokies' famous tourist attractions were spared, and both Gatlinburg and Pigeon Forge are as welcoming as before the fire.

Despite the total acreage burned, the fires created a "mosaic" landscape with some areas blackened and others left untouched. At press time only the summit of the Chimney Tops Trail remains closed, but park visitors will likely notice now softening road- and trail-side evidence of the fires for many years.

Zero Impact

Trails in the Great Smoky Mountains are heavily used year-round. We, as trail users and advocates, must be especially vigilant to make sure our passage leaves no lasting mark. Here are some rules for preserving park resources:

- Pack out all your own trash, including biodegradable items like orange peels. You might also pack out garbage left by less considerate hikers.

- Don't approach or feed any wild creatures—the red squirrel eyeing your snack food is best able to survive if it remains self-reliant.

- Don't pick wildflowers or gather rocks, antlers, feathers, and other treasures along the trail. Removing these items will take away from the next hiker's experience.

- Always stay on trail, to protect nature and avoid getting lost. This is also a good rule of thumb for avoiding poison oak, ivy, sumac, and stinging nettle, common regional trailside irritants.

- Don't cut switchbacks, which can promote erosion.

- Be courteous by not making loud noises while hiking or at viewpoints, picnic spots, or campsites.

- Many Smokies trails are multiuse, which means you'll share them with other hikers, equestrians, trail runners, and, in a few places, mountain bikers. Familiarize yourself with the proper trail etiquette, yielding the trail when appropriate.

- Use outhouses at trailheads or along the trail.

- Again, visit the park's website to investigate activities you may be interested in and to learn the latest regulations and policies.

How to Use This Guide

This guide is designed to be simple and easy to use. Each hike is described with a map and summary information that delivers the trail's vital statistics including length, difficulty, fees and permits, park hours, canine compatibility, trail contacts, and best hiking season. Directions to the trailhead are also provided, along with a general description of what you'll see along the way. A detailed route finder (Miles and Directions) sets forth mileages between significant landmarks along the trail, and more difficult hikes often include elevation gain.

This book divides the park into compass-direction quadrants. The Smokies' main ridge, basically the state line between Tennessee and North Carolina, roughly separates the park into northern and southern sections. The Newfound Gap Road, US 441 between Cherokee and Gatlinburg, cleaves the Smokies into eastern and western halves. Trails are thus featured in sections covering the northeast, southeast, southwest, and northwest parts of the park.

Difficulty Ratings

There are many easy hikes in this book, but easy is a relative term. Some would argue that no hike involving a climb is easy, but the Smokies are among the East's highest mountains, so heading uphill and down are facts of life. To aid in the selection of a hike that suits particular needs and abilities, each is rated easy, moderate, or more challenging. Bear in mind that even the most challenging routes can often be made easier by hiking within your limits, turning around when you've had enough, and taking rests when you need them.

Easy hikes are generally short and flat, taking no longer than an hour or so to complete.

Moderate hikes involve increased distance and relatively mild changes in elevation and will take one to two hours to complete.

More challenging hikes feature steep stretches and greater distances, generally take longer than two hours to complete, and can include a few of the park's more strenuous hikes among those recommended.

These are completely subjective ratings—consider that what you think is easy is entirely dependent on your level of fitness, sureness of foot, and the adequacy of your gear (primarily shoes or boots, and even hiking poles, for more rugged terrain). If you are hiking with a group, you should select a hike with a rating that's appropriate for the person in your party who is the least fit (and then be sure you don't set a blistering pace that exhausts them).

Approximate hiking times are based on the assumption that on flat ground, most walkers average 2 miles per hour. Adjust that rate by the steepness of the terrain and your level of fitness (subtract time if you're an aerobic animal and add time if you're hiking with kids), and you have a ballpark hiking duration. Be sure to add more time if you plan to picnic or take part in other activities like bird-watching or photography.

Finally, please note that some hikes in this "Best Easy" book are rated as "More Challenging." This book specifies those hikes because some are strenuous and difficult. Be aware of these ratings and be sure not to accidentally take a difficult trail. Why include more difficult hikes in this book? Because these trail descriptions help even the casual hiker appreciate how challenging the Smokies can be. In addition, any group of novice hikers often includes experienced, fit trail users who just might want to tackle the park's best adventures without buying another book. These hikes are for you! And if a less serious hiker wants to sample one of these trails, I often include a turnaround point where beginners can wave goodbye as the hard-core head higher.

Trail Finder

Best Hikes for Backpackers

13	The Boogerman Trail
14	Big Creek
18	Deep Creek Loop
11	Smokemont Self-Guiding Nature Trail and Loop

Best Hikes for Waterfalls

4	Grotto Falls
5	Ramsey Cascades
17	Juney Whank Falls
18	Deep Creek Loop
22	Abrams Falls

Best Hikes for Geology Lovers

7	Alum Cave Trail to Mount LeConte
20	Chimney Tops Trail

Best History Hikes

2	Sugarlands Valley Self-Guiding Nature Trail
3	Noah "Bud" Ogle Self-Guiding Trail
10	Oconaluftee River Trail/Mountain Farm Museum
12	Ferguson Cabin
13	The Boogerman Trail
21	Elkmont Self-Guiding Nature Trail

Best Hikes for Children

1	Quiet Walkways (Northeast Section)
2	Sugarlands Valley Self-Guiding Nature Trail
9	Quiet Walkways (Southeast Section)
10	Oconaluftee River Trail/Mountain Farm Museum
17	Juney Whank Falls

Best Hikes for Peak Baggers

Best Hikes for Great Views

Best Hikes for Nature Lovers

Map Legend

40	Interstate Highway
19	U.S. Highway
28	State Highway
	Local Road
	Unpaved Road
	Featured Trail
	Trail
	Paved Trail
	State Line
	River/Creek
	National Park
	Indian Reservation
🎭	Amphitheater
▲	Camping
⚇	Gate
❓	Information Center
⬛	Inn/Lodging
🗼	Observation Tower
🅿	Parking
▲	Peak
🎪	Picnic Area
■	Point of Interest/Structure
🏠	Ranger Station
🍴	Restaurant
🚻	Restroom
~○	Spring
○	Town
❶	Trailhead
✺	Viewpoint/Overlook
≋	Waterfall

Northeast Section

1 Quiet Walkways

The Smokies' "Quiet Walkways" are great offerings—short strolls through sylvan settings along the Newfound Gap Road and in other places. They lead to very easy glimpses of nature and are often less busy than trails to specific points of interest. Some tie in to existing trails, but most are segments of now-interrupted valley roads used by early settlers or loggers. These paths invite motorists to get out of their cars and stretch their legs, the perfect places to get into the woods for the permitted 15 minutes if you do not have the park's otherwise required parking pass (be sure to see the Introduction for more info). There are four of these walkways along Newfound Gap Road between the Sugarlands Visitor Center and Newfound Gap.

Distance: Short out-and-back strolls; up to 0.5 mile each

Hiking time: About 30 minutes each, unless you dawdle

Difficulty: Easy

Trail surface: Usually flat and firm, sometimes grassy

Other trail users: None; no dogs or horses allowed

Best season: Year-round except when covered in snow or ice

Canine compatibility: Dogs not permitted

Fees and permits: Parking tag/fee required if hiking more than 15 minutes (be sure to see Introduction)

Schedule: Closed only when inclement weather closes Newfound Gap Road

Trail contacts: Information about trails, camping, road closures, as well as downloadable maps and a "Smokies Trip Planner" is available online under the "Plan Your Visit" part of the park's excellent website, www.nps.gov/grsm. The park recommends calling the Backcountry Information Office as the preferred way to clarify camping regulations and ask trip-planning questions; open 8 a.m. to 5 p.m. daily, (865) 436-1297.

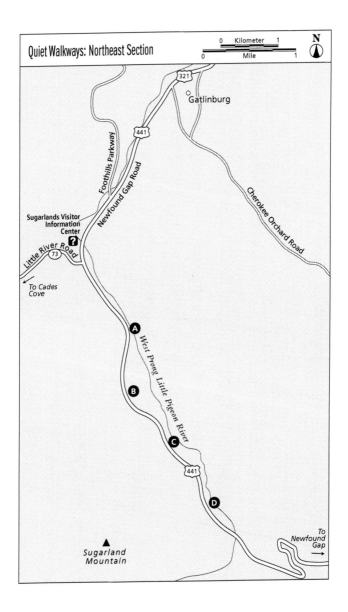

Quiet Walkways: Northeast Section

0   Kilometer   1

0   Mile   1

N

Gatlinburg

321

441

Foothills Parkway

Newfound Gap Road

Cherokee Orchard Road

Sugarlands Visitor
Information
Center

?

Little River Road

73

To Cades
Cove

West Prong Little Pigeon River

A

B

C

441

D

Sugarland
Mountain

To
Newfound
Gap

Finding the trailhead: Traveling south from Sugarlands Visitor Center, these paths are located on the left (east) at 1 mile, 1.7 miles, 2.2 miles, and 3.2 miles. Most are marked by small "Quiet Walkway" signs at the parking turnouts.

The Hikes

Hikers with a disabled placard or license plate can stroll all these paths without a parking tag. The first Quiet Walkway (at 1 mile) (A) explores a setting similar to the Sugarlands Nature Trail without the pavement or people. Bear right near the river to reach a nicely intact portion of the old valley road.

The walkway at 1.7 miles (B) has accessible parking for people with disabilities and leads down a gradual old road grade to a bench where the Little Pigeon River is visible below (this is a favorite for fishing).

The walkway at 2.2 miles (C) descends steeper switchbacks to the river and offers a rock-delineated section of the old road and evidence of early farming and settlement.

The walkway at 3.2 miles (D) forms a little loop. Dip down the graveled path and go right above the river along a spectacular stone wall. At a gap in the wall, go left to the river and back to close the loop by hiking up past a bench.

2 Sugarlands Valley Self-Guiding Nature Trail

This fully accessible trail is a must-see Smokies experience for even the hard-core hiker. It is very well done, with wonderfully informative interpretive plaques as well as tactile exhibits for people who are visually impaired. This path conveys the appeal of the well-watered, verdant valleys that drew so many settlers to the foot of these high mountains.

Distance: 0.5-mile loop
Hiking time: 30-45 minutes
Difficulty: Easy
Trail surface: Paved
Other trail users: None; no dogs or horses allowed
Best season: Early summer
Canine compatibility: Dogs not permitted
Fees and permits: Parking tag/fee required if hiking more than 15 minutes (be sure to see Introduction)

Schedule: Closed only when inclement weather closes Newfound Gap Road
Maps: USGS Gatlinburg; TOPO! Tennessee, Kentucky
Trail contacts: Information about trails, camping, road closures, as well as downloadable maps and a "Smokies Trip Planner" is available online under the "Plan Your Visit" part of the park's excellent website, www.nps.gov/grsm.
Special considerations: A nature trail brochure is available to buy at the trailhead.

Finding the trailhead: The trail starts on the east side of Newfound Gap Road, 0.4 mile south of Sugarlands Visitor Center and 13 miles north of Newfound Gap. GPS: N35 40.770' / W83 31.873'

The Hike

You'll be nicely acquainted with this and other Smokies lowland valley locations once you've traveled this trail. From the early 1800s, the rough road through Sugarlands Valley was the main route between Gatlinburg, or White Oak Flats, and the Cherokee area of North Carolina. Farms and communities spread up the lower sections of the valley, and logging here was lighter than at many places in what is now the park. In the 90 or so years since farmers, loggers, and even the first trickle of vacation-home builders left the fledgling national park, there's been a dramatic reclamation by nature.

The loop splits just past a bridge with an embedded bench. Go left (east) and two startling river-rock chimneys appear in the trail's first curves, all that remain of some of the Smokies' earliest vacation homes (circa 1900). Not far beyond, at brochure stop 3, a side shoot of the paved trail leads left (east), where the old road is particularly identifiable beside the West Prong Little Pigeon River as it rushes all along this side of the trail. This path's artfully weaving exploration of the terrain is itself an aesthetic experience. Keep your eyes peeled throughout this hike for evidence of other walls and rock piles—the trail passes right through one stout stone wall.

All along the trail, bas-relief plaques present opportunities for people who are visually impaired to touch the shapes of leaves, fish (more than sixty species are found in the park), salamanders (more here than in any other spot in North America), poison ivy, the deeply grooved bark of sourwood, and more.

The trail turns along the end of the loop at 0.3 mile and kids can easily step off and down to a small side stream

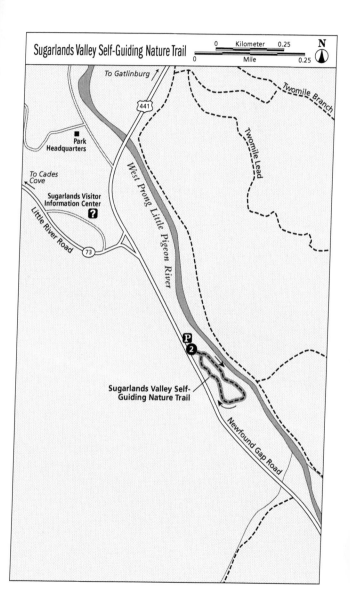

Sugarlands Valley Self-Guiding Nature Trail

0   Kilometer   0.25

0   Mile   0.25

N

To Gatlinburg

441

Twomile Branch

Twomile Lead

Park Headquarters

West Prong Little Pigeon River

To Cades Cove

Sugarlands Visitor Information Center

Little River Road

73

P
2

Sugarlands Valley Self-Guiding Nature Trail

Newfound Gap Road

running beneath the Newfound Gap Road not far away. As the loop nears its junction, one insightful sign shows the stages of forest recovery after settlement with a depiction of the scene beside the trail that includes the cabins that once stood by the chimneys in the distance.

If you'd like to see other defined sections of the old road across the Smokies, consider a few of the nearby quiet walkways or take the loftier Chimney Tops Trail. Where that trail turns right/west (at 0.9 mile), follow the Road Prong Trail left (south, and then east) as far as you care to walk.

3 Noah "Bud" Ogle Self-Guiding Trail

This great hike is recommended for easy roadside access to historic structures and a longer super-scenic streamside stretch that'll make you feel like you've walked into an early photo of hardscrabble backwoods life in the Smokies.

Distance: 0.8-mile loop
Hiking time: 1 hour or less
Difficulty: Easy
Trail surface: This trail is a snap if you just visit the buildings. But the longer loop of the path, though gradual, follows a rocky old road and crosses boulder gardens on a less-than-level stone pathway.
Other trail users: None
Best season: Spring or late fall/ winter, to either sense the promise of a new Smokies' planting season (and great wildflowers) or to grasp the bleaker prospect of months to go in these mountains without fresh food
Canine compatibility: Dogs not permitted
Fees and permits: Parking tag/ fee required if hiking more than 15 minutes (be sure to see Introduction)
Schedule: Open year-round, except rarely after snowfall and before plowing

Maps: USGS Le Conte; TOPO! Tennessee, Kentucky
Trail contacts: Information about trails, camping, road closures, as well as downloadable maps and a "Smokies Trip Planner" is available online under the "Plan Your Visit" part of the park's excellent website, www.nps.gov/grsm.
Special considerations: But there's more so don't turn around on Cherokee Orchard Road to get back to Gatlinburg—continue around the 5-mile one-way Roaring Fork Motor Nature Trail, one of the park's best motor tours (open mid-Mar to late Nov; no trailers, buses, or trucks allowed). A trailhead brochure is available, and turnouts enable stops that highlight historic structures and spectacular scenery. You'll also possibly glimpse wildlife, including bears. The Grotto Falls hike is also on this route.

Finding the trailhead: From US 441 in Gatlinburg, turn at traffic light #8 onto Historic Nature Trail/Airport Road. In 0.6 mile, keep right (southeast) at the junction, then stay straight on Cherokee Orchard Road. The trailhead is on the right (south) 2.6 miles from US 441. GPS: N35 41.008' / W83 29.423'

The Hike

Few visitors to the Smokies today would fail to agree that the decision to create the park was a wise one. Then again, no one alive now had to look back over their shoulder at a former home they had to abandon in what is today America's most visited national park. You can only imagine the plight of displaced residents. This trail movingly conveys the beauty of the place they left behind—and the investment needed to carve out a life there in the first place.

One of the displaced, Noah "Bud" Ogle, gazes at you from the trailhead sign. Luckily, if you're short for time, a breeze through his beautiful, handcrafted cabin and barn is only 100 yards from the trailhead. An old road grade rises to the left of the historic buildings. The 2016 fire crept alarmingly close to these structures.

To really savor this site, which means seeing the structures last, bear right (southwest) not far from the trailhead, before the log buildings, and follow the nature trail sign on an easy grade out into the woods. Beyond post #3 you'll cross a split log bridge and bear left past post #5 on an old road that linked Gatlinburg to local farms along boulder-strewn LeConte Creek.

At a trail junction, the Twin Creeks Trail heads right (northwest), leading 1.8 miles to Gatlinburg (add an out-and-back trek on this gradual path if you like). Beyond, the Bud Ogle trail dips down through a section of old road

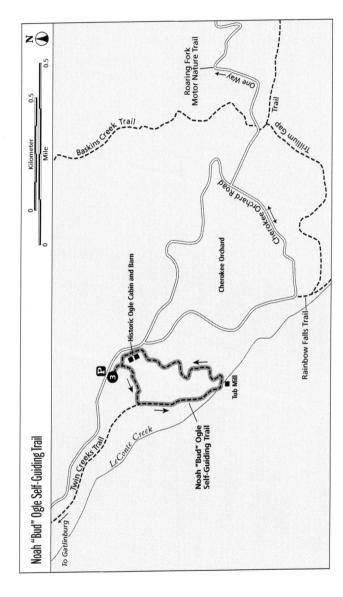

Noah "Bud" Ogle Self-Guiding Trail

N

Kilometer
0   0.5

Mile
0   0.5

To Gatlinburg

Twin Creeks Trail

LeConte Creek

P
3

Historic Ogle Cabin and Barn

Noah "Bud" Ogle
Self-Guiding Trail

Tub Mill

Cherokee Orchard

Cherokee Orchard Road

Rainbow Falls Trail

Baskins Creek Trail

Roaring Fork Motor Nature Trail

One Way

Trillium Gap Trail

lined with rock walls past post #7 and a huge pile of rocks, remnants of a cabin used to let young couples have a home until their own could be completed. Just beyond, an unusual evergreen cluster of tall skinny boxwoods further marks the home site. Off in the woods to the far right there's extensive evidence of other walls.

The trail swings left (south) up the creek past a stunning old tub mill sitting in a stream. Step inside if you like. The log flumes convey water down to strike the metal wheel (at one time enclosed in a "tub," hence the name). The Ogles used it to grind their own and neighbors' grain.

When the trail rises across a lush fern- and moss-covered rib of rocks and boulders scattered through the woods, you'll wonder how anyone could have farmed this area. Cross a bridge made of a massive log and at post #11, it's a lot easier to imagine that this area was a field of crops before the forest grew up.

You'll return to the farm buildings from above as you cross a small stream by the barn. Glance inside, then wander down the old road to the right. The water here was funneled to the farmhouse via log flumes. Explore the cabin, expanded as years went by on both sides of the fireplace (which was never quite fully enclosed to avoid the risk of fire).

Miles and Directions

0.0   Begin at the trailhead on the south side of Cherokee Orchard Road.

0.2   Reach the stone wall section of the old road.

0.4   Arrive at the tub mill.

0.8   Arrive back at the trailhead.

4 Grotto Falls

Grotto Falls, reached by the Trillium Gap Trail, is a place where anyone can experience the cinema fantasy of standing behind a waterfall (though don't expect to be completely hidden back here). Grotto Falls shoots off a semicircular ledge, and the trail artfully swings behind the cascade.

Distance: 2.6 miles out and back

Hiking time: 2–3 hours

Difficulty: Moderate

Trail surface: Packed soil with firm footing, but the clay sections can be slick after rain

Other trail users: Llama teams regularly use this trail (Mon, Wed, and Fri) to resupply Le Conte Lodge with food and necessities for guests, so you can arrange to see them padding along. They usually begin their trek by 8 a.m. and can often be seen returning from the lodge by 4 p.m. or so. To double-check the latest schedule, call (865) 429-5704. Check out the lodge's blog for up-to-date info on the llama trips; highonle conte.com.

Best season: Spring for flowers and stream flow. Also midweek; this is a popular trail.

Canine compatibility: Dogs not permitted

Fees and permits: Parking tag/fee required if hiking more than 15 minutes (be sure to see Introduction)

Schedule: Mid-Mar to late Nov

Maps: USGS Mount Le Conte; TOPO! Tennessee, Kentucky

Trail contacts: Information about trails, camping, road closures, as well as downloadable maps and a "Smokies Trip Planner" is available online under the "Plan Your Visit" part of the park's excellent website, www.nps.gov/grsm.

Special considerations: Grotto Falls is not far from Gatlinburg, and it's also on one of the busier trails to Mount Le Conte. If you want to avoid crowds, choose shoulder or off-seasons and arrive very early to find parking space in the lot.

Other: Reaching Grotto Falls requires driving the 5-mile one-way Roaring Fork Motor Nature Trail, one of the park's best motor tours (open from mid-Mar to late Nov; no trailers, buses, or trucks allowed). A trailhead brochure is available, and turnouts include historic structures and spectacular scenery. You may glimpse wildlife, including bears. The Noah "Bud" Ogle Self-Guiding Trail is also on this route.

Finding the trailhead: From US 441 in Gatlinburg, turn at traffic light #8 onto Historic Nature Trail/Airport Road. In 0.6 mile, keep right (southeast) at the junction, then stay straight on Cherokee Orchard Road. At 3.6 miles (1 mile past the Noah "Bud" Ogle nature trail parking area), turn right (east) onto the Roaring Fork Motor Nature Trail. The Grotto Falls Parking Area for the Trillium Gap Trail is on the left (north) 5.2 miles from US 441 (1.7 miles from the motor nature trail entrance). GPS: N35 40 49.540' / W83 27.750'

The Hike

Leave the lot amid a verdant old-growth forest of towering hemlocks now suffering from the park's infestation of the hemlock woolly adelgid. Go left (southeast) at the junction on the Trillium Gap Trail, 0.2 mile above the parking area. As the trail winds higher, it rises gradually through mature cove hardwood forest and delves into, then out of, the first stream crossing. That's a prominent feature of this trail—the way it weaves in and out around the dramatic leading ridges of Mount Le Conte, the park's single most massive summit.

The wet clay trail surface past the first stream—and in many spots on this route—can be slick when wet. The trail is so popular that roots across the path are worn flat. Nevertheless, choose an off-time and you can almost be alone. The grade grows much more gradual after the second stream

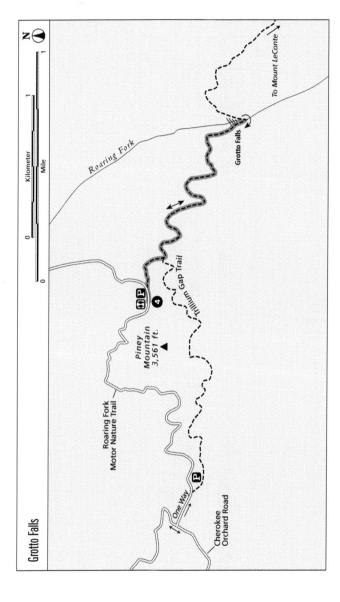

Grotto Falls

N

Roaring Fork

Kilometer

Mile

Roaring Fork
Motor Nature Trail

Piney
Mountain
3,561 ft. ▲

Trillium Gap Trail

4

Grotto Falls

To Mount LeConte

One Way

Cherokee
Orchard Road

crossing (one of five to the falls, if you're counting). The third easy stream hop presents a pretty little cascade in the crotch of the ridge, and at the fourth, the trees tower over a suddenly uniform understory of glossy green rhododendron. Out around the next ridge, the fifth stream drainage has the much deeper voice of a real cascade somewhere above. Soon you'll see a fine fall left of the trail with a deep pool. Farther above you'll see another cataract. Yep, that's Grotto Falls.

The trail rises to boulders at the falls' base and just beyond the trail winds behind the showering water. If you can catch this trail at a really off-time, the sight of the falls cascading into the rocky defile, devoid of hikers in bright outdoor gear, will recall nineteenth-century lithographs of America's romantic wilderness. Photo tip: This is the place to know how to use your shutter delay button so you don't have to hand-hold your camera. Whether you put the camera on a tripod or find a rock to set it on, a very slow shutter speed will create that milky blur that makes for such good waterfall photos.

Miles and Directions

0.0 Start by venturing into the old-growth hemlock forest.

0.2 Reach the junction with the Trillium Gap Trail and go left (southeast).

1.3 Arrive at Grotto Falls (the turnaround point).

2.6 Arrive back at the trailhead.

5 Ramsey Cascades

Reaching the Smokies' tallest (100 feet) and one of its most scenic waterfalls can't help but require a long, at times taxing day hike. The trip into this well-watered, rhododendron-rich watershed is made all the more special by one of the park's most impressive big forests.

Distance: 8 miles out and back

Hiking time: 5–7 hours

Difficulty: More challenging, with a gain of more than 2,000 feet to the falls

Trail surface: Starts on an old forest road then becomes a wooded trail. Major flooding in summer 2022 severely damaged the trail and access roads, but ongoing rehabilitation and improvement by the Trails Forever crew is expected to continue through late 2024. Like other trails in the park that have been rescued by trail maintainers, work on the Ramsey Cascades Trail includes new foot bridges, drainage culverts, wood and stone steps, and rerouted section of trail that should make this special hike even more enjoyable.

Other trail users: None; no dogs or horses allowed

Best season: Best in spring for flowers and for the falls after a rainy spell

Canine compatibility: Dogs not permitted

Fees and permits: Parking tag/fee required if hiking more than 15 minutes (be sure to see Introduction)

Schedule: Significant winter snow could restrict access.

Maps: USGS Mount Guyot; TOPO! Tennessee, Kentucky

Trail contacts: Information about trails, camping, road closures, as well as downloadable maps and a "Smokies Trip Planner" is available online under the "Plan Your Visit" part of the park's excellent website, www.nps.gov/grsm. The park recommends calling the Backcountry Information Office as the preferred way to clarify camping regulations and ask trip-planning questions; open 8 a.m. to 5 p.m. daily, (865) 436-1297. **Special considerations:** The Smokies are notorious for fatalities at waterfalls. Do not be tempted to climb this or any Smokies cascade.

Finding the trailhead: Leave Gatlinburg with a turn from US 441 onto eastbound US 321 at stoplight #3. In 6 miles, turn right (south) into the national park on Greenbrier Road. Follow the signs and the road goes gravel beyond the Greenbrier Ranger Station where you turn left (east) at the fork on Ramsey Prong Road. Continue; reach the trailhead at 4.7 miles. GPS: N35 42 10.290' / W83 21.417'

The Hike

Ramsey Cascades must have an identity crisis. Over the years it's been consistently spelled inconsistently, with either "sey" or "say" at the end. The current name, the correct spelling of the family who settled the area in 1800s, has stuck.

The trail's first 1.5 miles, on a very gradual forest road, makes a nice easy stroll without going all the way to the waterfall. The long bridge not far from the trailhead is another of those great Smokies opportunities to snag a photo from the middle of a rushing, wild stream amid lush rhododendron (the Boogerman Trail offers another such opportunity, also not far from the road).

Past the end of the dirt road, the route explores increasingly deep woods as the trail follows the Middle Prong of the Little Pigeon River. You'll cross a bridge at just more than 2 miles, then follow Ramsey Prong through dense, rich rhododendron forests that rise left (north) up to Greenbrier Pinnacle and right (south) up to Guyot Spur. This route through impressively towering trees delves deep into a cleft that runs all the way up to the Smokies' crest and Mount Guyot (6,621

Ramsey Cascades

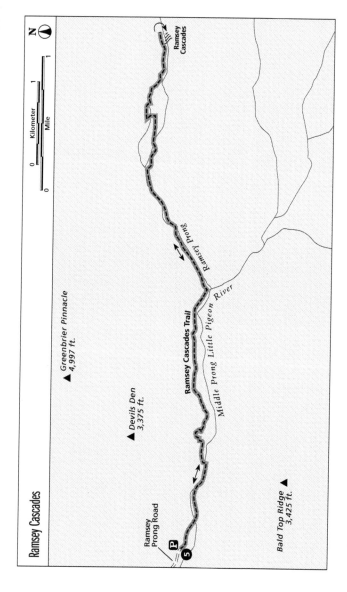

N

Greenbrier Pinnacle
4,997 ft.

Devils Den
3,375 ft.

Ramsey Cascades Trail

Ramsey Prong

Little Pigeon River

Middle Prong

Ramsey Cascades

Ramsey Prong Road

P

5

Bald Top Ridge
3,425 ft.

Kilometer

Mile

feet), the fourth highest peak in eastern America—second highest in the park and reputed to be the highest mountain in the East that does not have a formal trail to its summit.

At about 3 miles, cross a bridge to the left (north) bank of Ramsey Prong, and for the next 0.7 mile walk through an inspiring cove hardwood forest in an area that escaped the logger's saw. Big poplars dominate the forest. The final few tenths of a mile to the waterfall is steep, so prepare to take it easy and watch your footing. This waterfall is worth the effort.

Miles and Directions

0.0   Start on a gradual forest road.

1.5   Leave the dirt road on a woodsy trail.

3.0   Cross the last big bridge to the north side of Ramsey Prong.

4.0   Reach Ramsey Cascades.

8.0   Arrive back at the trailhead.

6 Appalachian Trail to Charlies Bunion with an Option to the Jumpoff

This walk on the storied Georgia-to-Maine footpath rises from Newfound Gap to fabulous views at craggy Charlies Bunion and includes a side trip to the Jumpoff.

Distance: 8.2 miles out and back to Charlies Bunion

Hiking time: Up to 7 hours

Difficulty: More challenging due to elevation gain (about 1,600 feet to Charlies Bunion), but the hike requires stamina and a sense of adventure due to the distance and rocky character of the Appalachian Trail (AT).

Trail surface: The slope is relatively gradual, but the trail is rocky and eroded in places.

Other trail users: None; no dogs or horses allowed

Best season: Winter, late fall, and early spring, as much for the lack of other hikers as for the fact that the arrival of high-pressure weather systems brings increased visibility to the colder seasons

Canine compatibility: Dogs not permitted

Fees and permits: Parking tag/fee required if hiking more than 15 minutes (be sure to see Introduction)

Schedule: Unavailable only when inclement weather closes Newfound Gap Road or snow and ice exceed your experience or gear

Maps: USGS Mount Le Conte and Mount Guyot; TOPO! Tennessee, Kentucky; TOPO! North Carolina, South Carolina

Trail contacts: Information about trails, camping, road closures, as well as downloadable maps and a "Smokies Trip Planner" available online under the "Plan Your Visit" part of the park's excellent website, www.nps.gov/grsm. The park recommends calling the Backcountry Information Office as the preferred way to clarify camping regulations and ask trip-planning questions; open 8 a.m. to 5 p.m. daily, (865) 436-1297.

Special considerations: Be prepared to see a lot of other hikers. Aim for an early start on an off-season weekday.

Other: This is one of a few hikes in this book that is not easy, but it is included because it is among the high-adventure hikes often hiked by well-equipped, motivated novices in good shape.

Finding the trailhead: The major trailhead parking area is on Newfound Gap Road, 13 miles from Sugarlands Visitor Center south of Gatlinburg in Tennessee, and 16 miles from Oconaluftee Visitor Center north of Cherokee, North Carolina. Leave the north side of the parking lot just beyond the trail to the restrooms. GPS: N35 36.663' / W83 25.493'

The Hike

Newfound Gap may be a truly popular place to start a hike, but this trailhead is also the best way to reach a few of the Smokies' most spectacular viewpoints. From the memorial to the Rockefeller Foundation, whose funds helped found the park (President Franklin Delano Roosevelt dedicated the park here in 1940), day hikes reach two awesome views: Charlies Bunion and the optional Jumpoff.

Leaving the gap, the trail was one of the first built-from-scratch sections of the AT, artfully excavated by the Civilian Conservation Corps. Though gradual, it's now badly eroded, rocky, and rooty in places as it rises from gap to gap, past the Sweat Heifer Creek Trail on the right (southeast) at 1.7 miles, to reach The Boulevard Trail on the left (northwest) at 2.7 miles. The Boulevard is a sharp evergreen ridge that leads 5.4 miles to the summit of Mount LeConte (6,593 feet), home to LeConte Lodge, open from late March into November, and the Mount LeConte shelter.

To reach the optional Jumpoff (6,100 feet), go left (northwest) on The Boulevard Trail a short distance and turn right (north) at the trail sign, heading up the rocky start. The trail

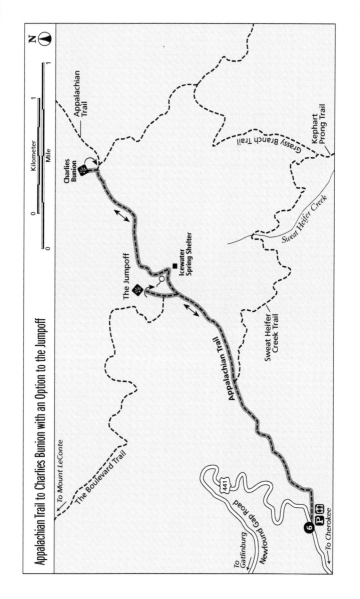

Appalachian Trail to Charlies Bunion with an Option to the Jumpoff

N

Kilometer

Mile

Appalachian Trail

Charlies Bunion

The Jumpoff

Icewater Spring Shelter

Appalachian Trail

To Mount LeConte

The Boulevard Trail

Sweat Heifer Creek Trail

Sweat Heifer Creek

Grassy Branch Trail

Kephart Prong Trail

To Gatlinburg

Newfound Gap Road

441

P

6

To Cherokee

crosses 6,150-foot Mount Kephart to a cliff-top view that looks down more than 1,000 feet and out east to Charlies Bunion. Mount Kephart honors twentieth-century author Horace Kephart, an early proponent of the park, whose book *Our Southern Highlanders* is highly recommended for Smokies visitors. (**Option**: For a shorter 6.5-mile round-trip hike, avoiding Charlies Bunion, return to the AT, turn right, and continue back to Newfound Gap.)

One of the most scenic sections of trail in the Smokies leads beyond the Boulevard Trail junction to Charlies Bunion. Continuing north on the AT (left if you turn from The Boulevard Trail), the trail to Icewater Spring Shelter appears on the right (east) in 0.3 mile. At about 4.0 miles (from Newfound Gap), the two rocky peaks that make up Charlies Bunion testify to the devastation that logging, forest fires, and subsequent floods caused before the park existed. All three denuded this area before 1930, and today the sparse vegetation makes the crags appear almost alpine. Go left at 4.0 miles for 0.1 mile to this truly spectacular—but lamentably named—beauty spot. The round-trip hike is about 8.2 miles.

Miles and Directions

0.0 Start from Newfound Gap on the AT.

1.7 Pass the Sweat Heifer Creek Trail on the right (southeast).

2.7 Reach the junction with The Boulevard Trail. (**Option**: Go left (northwest) here, then right (north) for the Jumpoff. It is 1 mile out and back from this intersection to the viewpoint and 6.5 miles round-trip from the Newfound Gap trailhead.)

3.0 Continuing on the AT, the path to Icewater Spring Shelter goes right (east).

4.0 Head left (north) to Charlies Bunion.

8.2 Arrive back at the trailhead.

7 Alum Cave Trail to Mount LeConte

Mount LeConte is the park's most spectacular peak, and the cozy accommodations of LeConte Lodge, not to mention bountiful (but simple) meals, make an overnight on this mountain one of eastern America's real adventures. It's not easy, but because there's food and a warm bed waiting on top, this memorable hike is often tackled by well-equipped, motivated novices in good shape. It'd be a lot more difficult if you were backpacking!

Distance: 10 miles out and back

Hiking time: 4–5 hours up, 2–3 hours down

Difficulty: More challenging, with an elevation gain of more than 2,600 feet

Trail surface: Rocky, steep forest trail that can have ice and snow in spots in spring and fall and deep drifts in winter

Other trail users: None

Best season: Whenever you can get a reservation—but be sure to avoid very early and late in the year unless you love and can handle cold, snow, and ice.

Canine compatibility: Dogs not permitted

Fees and permits: Parking tag/fee required if hiking more than 15 minutes (be sure to see Intro-

duction); fee for lodge accommodations

Schedule: Unavailable only when inclement weather closes Newfound Gap Road or snow and ice exceed your experience or gear. LeConte Lodge open from late Mar to late Nov.

Maps: USGS Mount LeConte; TOPO! Tennessee, Kentucky

Trail contacts: Information about trails, camping, road closures, as well as downloadable maps and a "Smokies Trip Planner" is available online under the "Plan Your Visit" part of the park's excellent website, www.nps.gov/grsm. The park recommends calling the Backcountry Information Office as the preferred way to clarify camping regulations and ask trip-planning questions; open 8 a.m. to 5 p.m. daily, (865) 436-1297. LeConte Lodge: (865) 429-5704; www.leconte-lodge.com, reservations@leconte-lodge.com. Also check out the lodge's blog: highonleconte.com.

Special considerations: This is one of a few hikes in this book that is bona fide strenuous but was selected because the route is the easiest way to tackle a high-adventure hike. Do not undertake this trek lightly but know that it is often hiked by well-prepared hikers in good shape. Get to the trailhead early.

Other: Special weather warning—expect potentially severe weather. You'll sleep in a propane-heated cabin, but flatlanders should bring layered, weatherproof garments (a hat and gloves included).

Finding the trailhead: The big Alum Cave parking areas lie on the east side of Newfound Gap Road 8.8 miles south from the Sugarlands Visitor Center and 4.4 miles north of Newfound Gap. Adding The Boulevard Trail option requires spotting a car at Newfound Gap (where restrooms are available). GPS: N35 37.730' / W83 27.051'

The Hike

The trek to Tennessee's LeConte Lodge is the Great Smokies' only true "hut hike," a generic term for experiences elsewhere in the United States and the world where you carry a light pack and find meals and overnight accommodations in a mountain hostel, lodge, or rustic hotel. It's great fun.

Mount LeConte and its lodge are a premier experience, so much so that many, many regulars come back year after year to test their fitness against the march of time. Just the lodge's popularity makes it difficult to book lodging. Getting reservations may not be easy, especially on weekends and holidays, but it's worth the effort. Flexibility helps. Your best bet is to e-mail (or fax/mail) the reservation form before "reservations open for the year," generally in early October for the following year (the lodge is open late March to just before Thanksgiving). Calling after the reservation "opening" date is also an option. Just hit "redial" and devote some time to getting through. If you want to get in, you may need to take any date that is available. If no reservations are available, ask to get on the waiting list. The closer you are to first on the list, the more likely you are to get in, so call early in the day. The list is maintained in 30-day time frames, so if you don't make the cut, you need to re-reserve for the next 30 days.

Hikers who get a reservation and use this style of back-country lodging carry relatively light packs, with clothing, toiletries, and snacks, and the "hut" provides a bed and meals. Guests at LeConte stay in cabins, some of which can accommodate one or a few families. There are flush toilets (no showers) and a dining building, where guests enjoy hearty meals that can include wine, and a separate relaxation lodge with board games and more.

Head out on one of the Smokies' most memorable hikes by crossing the first of many impressive log bridges that will carry you across the streams that enliven the lower half of this trail. Past the second bridge across Alum Cave Creek, the gradual, steadily rising Alum Cave Trail turns left (north) into the Styx Branch drainage and then swings out to Arch Rock at 1.4 miles. Crossing a few new bridges, built in 2021, below the cleft, the trail turns left (southwest) and climbs through a large arch of eroded rock on a steep curving flight of impressive stone steps (thanks to the Trails Forever trail crew). Leaving Styx Branch, the trail reaches the apex of the ridge and great views at Inspiration Point. Not far beyond, the massive overhang of Alum Cave Bluffs towers overhead at 2.3 miles. It's a short but steep climb along and under its sheltering brow, again on impressive wood stairways from the Trails Forever program (among many recent improvements on this trail). (**Option**: Turn around here for a 4.6-mile hike to one of the park's scenic high points.) A worthwhile interpretive brochure to this lower part of the trail is available at the sign near the trailhead parking lot.

From the bluffs on, LeConte rears up and the trail becomes a ridge walk suitable to a major summit. Views open above to the mountain's four peaks. Some of the most exciting terrain arrives as you slab left (west) from the ridge to carve across the high flank of the summit, at times through grassy landslides and across ledges with cables strung along the rock for safety. You'll sigh with relief as the trail levels through spruce and fir, passes the junction with the Rainbow Falls Trail on the left (north), and reveals the lodge's collection of cabins to the left (northeast).

Nearby viewpoints beckon. Cliff Top is the closest to the lodge and looks west to the sunset. Where the steps descend left to the lodge, the trail to Cliff Top goes right (west) so you will hike this loop counterclockwise. It reaches a great view, a suitable "summit view" for this entire hike, where sedge grasses grow down the cliff face to the right, and the parking area of Newfound Gap is far off to the left (southwest). The trail then loops left (east) and joins The Boulevard Trail beyond the lodge. Myrtle Point, farther beyond—in fact, past the mountain's highest summit, which has no view—looks east toward the sunrise. Both Cliff Top and Myrtle Point are ritual excursions for lodge guests. Looking west may be best, so call Cliff Top the high point for your hike if you're ready to head back the way you came.

The elevation drop from LeConte to Gatlinburg is impressive—it's a very direct vertical mile from the summit. That kind of relief is found in the Rockies more often than the Appalachians.

Miles and Directions

0.0 Start by heading east from the parking lot on the Alum Cave Trail.

1.4 Reach Arch Rock.

2.3 Arrive at Alum Cave Bluffs, a potential turnaround spot.

5.0 Reach the crest of Mount LeConte.

10.0 Arrive back at the trailhead.

Option

If your party has two cars (and you can meet the early parking challenge at two trailheads) or you can arrange a shuttle, start or end a 13.2-mile summit loop at Newfound Gap by walking the 5.4-mile evergreen knife-edge ridge of The Boulevard Trail, one of the most spectacular experiences in the park. Starting from Newfound Gap (at 5,048 feet, versus 3,800 feet at the Alum Cave Trail parking area), this is a longer route to the lodge (8.1 miles). It involves less of a climb but is probably more strenuous (considering the climb to the LeConte summit). You could also leave LeConte and descend The Boulevard Trail to the AT (at 2.7 miles from Newfound Gap); turn right (southwest) on the AT and continue to Newfound Gap, an 8.1-mile exit. The significant drawbacks

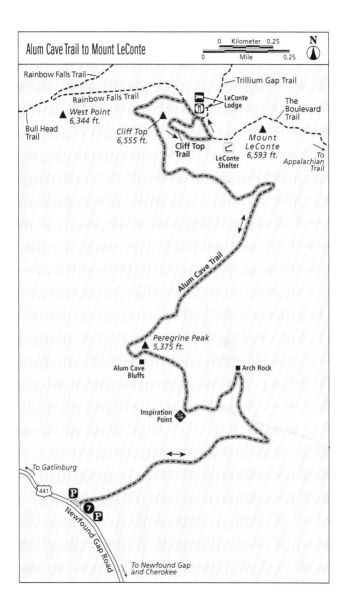

Alum Cave Trail to Mount LeConte

Kilometer 0.25
Mile 0.25
N

Rainbow Falls Trail
Trillium Gap Trail
Rainbow Falls Trail
LeConte Lodge
The Boulevard Trail
West Point 6,344 ft.
Bull Head Trail
Cliff Top 6,555 ft.
Cliff Top Trail
Mount LeConte 6,593 ft.
LeConte Shelter
To Appalachian Trail

Alum Cave Trail

Peregrine Peak 5,375 ft.
Alum Cave Bluffs
Arch Rock
Inspiration Point

To Gatlinburg
441
P
7
P
Newfound Gap Road

To Newfound Gap and Cherokee

in that direction are that The Boulevard Trail ends with a cruelly steep climb to the AT. And the AT, though not steep on the way down to Newfound Gap, is eroded, rocky, and not an easy walk. Nevertheless, The Boulevard Trail is one of the park's high points. It crosses an amazing landslide, with a cable to hang onto, not far below LeConte's peak. This wonderfully designed and well-maintained trail is almost always on the crest of a memorably sharp ridge.

Truth is, to this writer, the hike up and down Alum Cave Trail is the easiest way to see LeConte.

8 Cosby Self-Guiding Nature Trail

This trail is much more than a campground leg-stretcher. The designer of this trail must have been an artist. The way the trail offers up the old-growth forest experience is almost as impressive as the setting itself.

Distance: 1-mile loop
Hiking time: 1 hour plus
Difficulty: Easy
Trail surface: Packed soil or gravel with some rocky sections and old asphalt
Other trail users: None; no dogs or horses allowed
Best season: Year-round
Canine compatibility: Dogs not permitted
Fees and permits: Parking tag/fee required if hiking more than 15 minutes (be sure to see Introduction)
Schedule: Significant winter snow could restrict access.
Maps: USGS Hartford; TOPO! Tennessee, Kentucky

Trail contacts: Information about trails, camping, road closures, as well as downloadable maps and a "Smokies Trip Planner" is available online under the "Plan Your Visit" part of the park's excellent website, www.nps.gov/grsm.
Special considerations: This trail is so nice that you might consider camping at Cosby Campground just to hike it. In 2010, Great Recession stimulus funding repaved the campground for the first time since the 1960s. With other improvements, it's one of the best-maintained campgrounds in the park.

Finding the trailhead: From the US 321/TN 32 junction, about 15.4 miles east of Gatlinburg, turn right (southeast) and drive 1.2 miles. Turn right (south) again on the signed Cosby Campground road. Drive 2 miles and take the first left into the picnic area as you approach the campground. Swing along past the picnic sites (where restrooms and water are available seasonally) and up to the right into the hikers' parking area, just below the campground entrance kiosk. GPS: N35 45.361' / W83 12.475'

The Hike

This amble not far from the drainage of Crying Creek is so scenic it could almost bring tears to your eyes. Drop past the mileage sign to an atmospheric, old road grade and go right (south) on the Low Gap Trail, following the "Nature Trail" sign. Fine views look down onto the rushing stream in a mature cove hardwood forest. Pass the side trail on the right to the amphitheater parking area (actually the "formal" start of the nature trail, where the trail brochure is available at a trailhead dispenser). Continue below the nicely refurbished amphitheater to cross a ford on the old road at the trail's first numbered post.

Go left (east) past the ford to cross two log bridges and wander down between streams in a tall forest alive with water. This is the inspiring grove you were earlier looking down upon—a richly tangled and towering forest lush with ferns and moss. Also notice the extensive growths of partridgeberry that thrive along this trail. The plant (with many medicinal uses for Native Americans) flowers in early spring (with twin blossoms) and enlivens a winter hike with mats of small evergreen leaves and red autumn berries that feed wildlife throughout the cold season.

As you wander down and to the right among wet and dry drainages, old remnants of asphalt paving crop up. On the left, past post #4, sits a startlingly intertwined maple and birch—both germinated atop a fallen log that long ago decayed, leaving them standing on stiltlike roots. More streams appear to the right (east) and the trail crosses two more bridges.

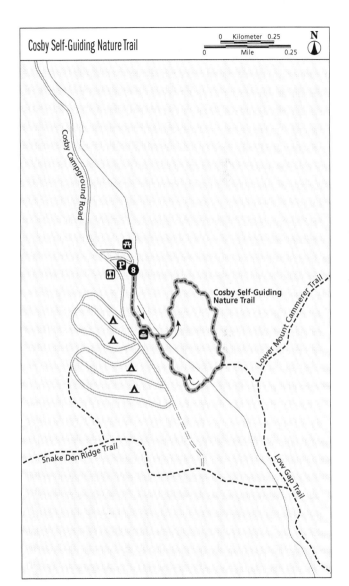

Cosby Self-Guiding Nature Trail

Cosby Campground Road

Lower Mount Cammerer Trail

Low Gap Trail

Snake Den Ridge Trail

Kilometer 0.25

Mile 0.25

N

Turning uphill, there's a trailside view of a little pool and cascade. Wandering higher between streams, amid a truly impressive cathedral of trees, the trail crosses another log bridge. There's no numbered post here, but if there were one it'd be labeled "Fallen Giant" in the trail brochure. A mammoth uprooted hardwood lies directly across the trail, nicely sawed to permit passage. At post #8, a rock-wall enclosure sits to the left and a fallen chimney scatters to the right. Beyond, the trail follows a moss-covered stone wall that also leads to a stream on the right. Imagine living in such a place.

At a T junction with the Low Gap Trail, go right (west), across two log bridges to the old road grade you started on. Turn right, descending past the amphitheater to the trailhead.

Miles and Directions

0.0 Start on the old road grade.

0.2 Turn left (northeast) from the old road onto the nature trail.

0.7 Turn right (southwest) at the junction with the Low Gap Trail.

1.0 Arrive back at the trailhead.

⑨ Quiet Walkways

The Smokies' Quiet Walkways are great offerings—short strolls through sylvan settings along the Newfound Gap Road and other locations. They lead to very easy glimpses of nature and are often less busy than trails to specific points of interest. Some tie in to existing trails but most are segments of now interrupted old roads used by settlers or loggers. These paths invite motorists to stretch their legs and return, the perfect places to get into the woods for the permitted 15 minutes if you do not have the park's otherwise required parking pass (be sure to see the Introduction for more info). There are five along Newfound Gap Road between the Oconaluftee Visitor Center and Newfound Gap.

Distance: Short out-and-back strolls; up to 0.5 mile each
Hiking time: 30 minutes max, unless you dawdle
Difficulty: Easy
Trail surface: Flat and firm, sometimes grassy
Other trail users: None; no dogs or horses allowed
Best season: Year-round, except when covered with snow or ice
Canine compatibility: Dogs not permitted
Fees and permits: Parking tag/fee required if hiking more than 15 minutes (be sure to see Introduction)
Schedule: Closed only when inclement weather closes Newfound Gap Road
Maps: TOPO! North Carolina, South Carolina
Trail contacts: Information about trails, camping, road closures, as well as downloadable maps and a "Smokies Trip Planner" is available online under the "Plan Your Visit" part of the park's excellent website, www.nps.gov/grsm.

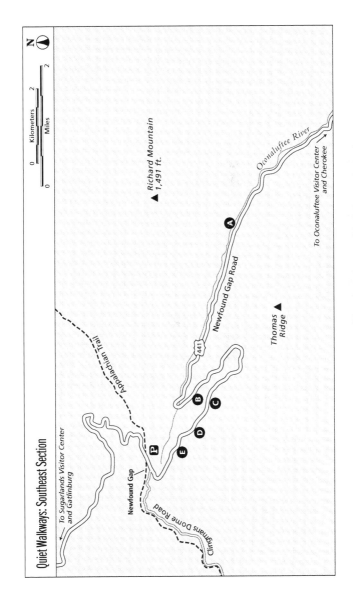

Quiet Walkways: Southeast Section

N

0   Kilometers   2

0   Miles   2

Richard Mountain
1,491 ft.

Oconaluftee River

To Oconaluftee Visitor Center
and Cherokee

Newfound Gap Road

A

441

Thomas Ridge

B

C

D

E

P

Newfound Gap

Appalachian Trail

To Sugarlands Visitor Center
and Gatlinburg

Clingmans Dome Road

Finding the trailhead: Driving north on Newfound Gap Road (US 441) from Oconaluftee Visitor Center, these paths are located at 7.4 miles, 10.9 miles, 13.7 miles, 14.1 miles, and 14.4 miles. Most are marked by small "Quiet Walkway" signs at the parking turnouts.

The Hikes

Hikers with a disabled placard or license plate can stroll all these paths without a parking tag. The first Quiet Walkway in this section of the park (at 7.4 miles on the right) (A) steeply enters the woods, quickly reaching Beech Flats Prong.

The walkway at 10.9 miles on the right (B) is a long stretch of the old Newfound Gap Road, the earliest paved road across the park that was closed when a more gradual section of the road was built.

The walkway on the left at 13.7 miles (C) runs along a ridge top perpendicular to the road. Turn around when it heads down. The walkway on the left at 14.1 miles (D) dips into the Deep Creek drainage among northern hardwoods at 4,700 feet.

The loftiest and last walkway, on the left at 14.4 miles (E) and just a little more than 1 mile from the Clingmans Dome Road and Newfound Gap, also zigzags down along the ridge into Deep Creek with occasional views.

10 Oconaluftee River Trail/ Mountain Farm Museum

The Mountain Farm Museum may just be a stroll, but combine it with one of the Smokies' best-kept-secret easy walks, the Oconaluftee River Trail, and you have one of the park's best combinations of scenery and interpretation. It is a masterful meshing of insight into Native Americans and later settlers, the perfect outdoor add-on to the exhibits at the Oconaluftee Visitor Center.

Distance: Up to 3 miles out and back from the Oconaluftee Visitor Center to Cherokee, with shorter out-and-back options from Newfound Gap Road trailheads to the Mountain Farm Museum

Hiking time: About 2 hours plus 30-minute shortcut options

Difficulty: Very easy to moderate, depending on length

Trail surface: Grassy at Mountain Farm, lightly graveled road-width path

Other trail users: The Oconaluftee River Trail is one of the very few trails in the Smokies where dogs and bikes are permitted; neither OK at Mountain Farm (but riders and dog walkers can avoid the farm enclosure).

Best season: Year-round

Canine compatibility: Dogs are permitted on the Oconaluftee River Trail while on leash—but no dogs are allowed in the Mountain Farm Museum enclosure.

Fees and permits: Parking tag/ fee required if hiking more than 15 minutes (be sure to see Introduction)

Schedule: Year-round. Even when inclement weather closes Newfound Gap Road, this trail can be hiked from the Cherokee trailhead. Summer and fall are great due to the costumed interpretation of mountain life at the farm museum.

Maps: USGS Smokemont and Whittier; TOPO! North Carolina, South Carolina

Trail contacts: Information about trails, camping, road closures, as well as downloadable maps and a "Smokies Trip Planner" is available online under the "Plan Your Visit" part of the park's excellent website, www.nps.gov/grsm.

Special considerations: This hike can be started from a variety of trailheads, making it customizable for different distances and fitness levels.

Finding the trailhead: Park at the Oconaluftee Visitor Center (where restrooms and water are available), at the Cherokee Transit parking area in Cherokee, or at any of three pull-offs between Cherokee and the Oconaluftee Visitor Center on the right side of Newfound Gap Road. Driving north from the park boundary at Cherokee, those parking spots are located at 0.3 mile (a turnout at the park entrance sign), at 0.5 mile (a parking pull-off), and at 0.7 mile where there's a single car parking spot at the start of the Blue Ridge Parkway. To reach that, turn right/northeast from Newfound Gap Road onto the Parkway, turn around at the first overlook, and on the way back to Newfound Gap Road, pull off the parkway to the right onto roadside gravel just across the bridge from milepost 469. Oconaluftee Visitor Center trailhead GPS: N35 30.786' / W83 18.398'

The Hike

If you've ever wondered what a hog does when an overspreading oak drops a September acorn into its artfully sited sty, this trail can answer that question.

I may be overly fond of this path, in part because the route suggested combines two separate experiences that most visitors don't usually combine.

The Mountain Farm Museum is a flat, 0.5-mile wander among a stunning collection of nineteenth-century backcountry farm structures that paint a vivid picture of a settler's life, complete with chickens crowing and pigs grunting (in season). The Oconaluftee River Trail (ORT) leads from the farm to Cherokee—or from Cherokee to the farm. Hiking either way offers a major dose of riverside scenery along with one of the park's best insights into Cherokee Indian culture. A half dozen interpretive plaques on the trail explain Cherokee beliefs and respect for the natural world (in English and Cherokee). The signs include evocative illustrations by Cherokee artists that will make you want to visit the tribe's Qualla Arts and Crafts gallery in town. There's a bench at each sign and at other places along the path.

Above the visitor center the river flows narrow and fast along Newfound Gap Road, but along the ORT, the Oconaluftee spreads wide and dances brightly over ledges and around islands. The river starts in one of the East's biggest wilderness areas and the refreshing clean smell of the water matches the emerald-green color in a way that defies verbal description.

All along the river there's an open understory of grasses and ferns with many wildflowers, including bee balm and entire trailside borders of jewelweed or touch-me-not (in late August; see this book's front cover photo).

One reason the ORT is a good family hike for visitors is that it's very popular with Cherokees as a place to jog or stroll with family. Seeing local Native Americans enjoying their ancestral homeland while you pause to read interpretive signs about Cherokee legend is a rich experience.

Leave the visitor center's south side and the trail splits; go left (east) to the Mountain Farm Museum while to the right (southeast) the Oconaluftee River Trail skirts the farm for about the same distance. Explore the farm first—interpretive signs explain the structures, all gathered in 1950 from throughout the Smokies, and also show pictures of many buildings in their original locations. After you've toured the farm, exit past the Apple House near the cornfield and turn left (southeast) on the ORT. The trail follows the farm's fence line, then swings close to the river at the first Cherokee cultural sign.

At 0.7 mile the trail goes under the Blue Ridge Parkway bridge and side steps lead right (south) to a roadside parking slip (one of three places to park along the ORT that permit shorter out-and-back hikes from the roadside to the Mountain Farm Museum and back—the reverse of the direction described here). The trail swings away from the river and at 0.9 mile crosses a small bridge where a right (west) turn up the bank just beyond leads to the second roadside trailhead, this one a designated parking area on Newfound Gap Road. At 1.2 miles from the Mountain Farm Museum, a rock wall leads right (west) to the next roadside trailhead at the park's major entrance sign (the first parking spot reached from Cherokee). The trail then crosses Big Cove Road at 1.3 miles and reaches the sidewalks of Cherokee across from the Cherokee Transit parking area at the reservation boundary at 1.5 miles.

By the way—when the acorns drop into the pig sty, the pig trots right to them!

Miles and Directions

- **0.0** Start at the Oconaluftee Visitor Center.
- **0.7** Pass side steps to the Blue Ridge Parkway.
- **1.2** Pass the park entrance sign.
- **1.5** Reach the Cherokee Transit parking area and turnaround point.
- **3.0** Arrive back at the trailhead at the Oconaluftee Visitor Center.

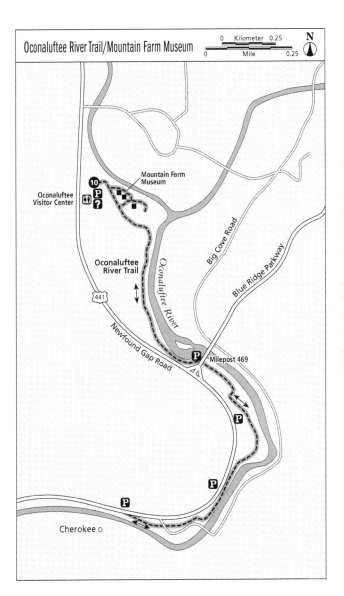

Oconaluftee River Trail/Mountain Farm Museum

Mountain Farm Museum

Oconaluftee Visitor Center

Oconaluftee River Trail

Oconaluftee River

Big Cove Road

Blue Ridge Parkway

Newfound Gap Road

441

Milepost 469

Cherokee

Options

If you don't want to start at the visitor center, choose the roadside parking area that's right for you and hike out-and-back to make a little end loop of the Mountain Farm Museum and ORT. From the Cherokee Transit lot, the round-trip hike to the museum is 3 miles (the same distance as from the visitor center to Cherokee and back). The round-trip hike to the museum is 2.4 miles from the park entrance sign, 1.8 miles from the parking area near the trail bridge (immediately before the sign "Blue Ridge Parkway Next Right"), and 1.4 miles from the roadside slip at the start of the Blue Ridge Parkway. From all of these starting points (see "Finding the trailhead" for road directions), you begin with Cherokee culture, in a scenic, natural setting, and end with the newcomers.

11 Smokemont Self-Guiding Nature Trail and Loop

One of the park's steeper nature trails rises above Smokemont Campground, site of one of the Smokies' biggest, early-twentieth-century logging operations. A few longer options include a loop and a very easy overnighter for beginner backpackers.

Distance: 0.75-mile lollipop loop (nature trail); 6.1-mile loop; 3.6-mile backpacking option

Hiking time: About 30 minutes for the nature trail, 3 hours for the loop

Difficulty: Easy for nature trail/moderate for loop

Trail surface: Packed clay soil surface, with a very rooty upper section on the nature trail. For the loop, the hike starts on a gravel road and ends on a steeper forest trail.

Other trail users: The Bradley Fork Trail, Chasteen Creek Trail, and campsite 50 are open to equestrian traffic.

Best season: Spring for wildflowers (on the loop)

Canine compatibility: Dogs not permitted

Fees and permits: Parking tag/fee required if hiking more than 15 minutes (be sure to see Introduction)

Schedule: Closed only when inclement weather closes Newfound Gap Road. Smokemont Campground is open year-round.

Maps: USGS Smokemont; TOPO! North Carolina, South Carolina

Trail contacts: Information about trails, camping, road closures, as well as downloadable maps and a "Smokies Trip Planner" is available online under the "Plan Your Visit" part of the park's excellent website, www.nps.gov/grsm. Since 2013, backcountry campers have been required to have advance reservations and a permit for all overnight camping in the park (a fee is charged).

The Smokies is a very popular backpacking destination, so the park's regulations are extensive and policies differ for General Backcountry Permits and AT Thru-Hiker Permits. If you want to reserve campsite 50, visit the park's permit and reservation website (https://smokiespermits .nps.gov) for further information and to process your permit. The park recommends calling the Backcountry Information Office as the preferred way to clarify camping regulations and ask trip-planning questions; open 8 a.m. to 5 p.m. daily, (865) 436-1297. **Special considerations:** You'll need to reserve a spot in advance at campsite 50 if you plan to do the optional 3.6-mile out-and-back backpacking trip (see above).

Finding the trailhead: Heading north on Newfound Gap Road, turn right (north) into Smokemont Campground, located 3.2 miles north of Oconaluftee Visitor Center. Cross the river bridge to the T junction and go left. Pass the campground check-in kiosk and not far beyond, turn left and park on the right opposite campsites B31 and B32 (restrooms are available just beyond, on the left, by campsite B36). To reach the start of the Smokemont Loop, either pass the nature trail and park on the right at an old bridge or drive farther into the campground and where the D loop splits, take the left fork for sites D20 to D45. Park at the end of the loop near campsite D32 at the "Bradley Fork Trail" sign (restrooms are available near campsite D29 just south of the trailhead). When you finish the loop hike, you'll need to walk back through the campground to wherever you parked. In winter, with D loop and its restroom closed, the recommended parking spot is near the nature trail at the old bridge, not far from watchful ranger offices near the campground entrance. Nature trail trailhead GPS: N35 33.465' / W83 18.742'

The Hike

The Smokemont Nature Trail starts at a roadside sign and crosses three single log bridges that impart a deep woods Smokies feel. The second bridge spans lively, cacophonous Bradley Fork, and the third crosses a silent, lazy side flow that could almost be another creek in a completely different place. Beyond, the trail slams into a sharp hillside and splits, each side rising steeply to wrap around the knob above.

Go right (north) and the trail undulates up along a very steep side hill overlooking the campground. No flat little loop this: You're immediately up and out of the campground in a place that's suddenly not so tame. An irony, given that the campground occupies the site of an early twentieth-century logging village that denuded the surrounding mountainsides, causing devastating fires and floods. The trail's brochure recounts the destruction and recovery at twelve posts along the way.

The trail climbs to the right then switchbacks left just below the peak of the knob on rooty footing through rhododendron and mountain laurel. When the path slides onto a ridgetop beyond, you'll sniff wood smoke from campfires being drawn through the gap, while right-hand views open up to the high Smokies (with a bench).

Running down the ridge, the trail veers right (north) off the back of the knob, then left (south) through mountain laurel and white pines above the emerging sound of a stream and traffic on Newfound Gap Road. A sign points left (north) on the nature trail where an informal side trail leaves to the right (a connector to the Smokemont Loop Trail). The main nature trail swings left (north) across the lower face of the knob to a right (east) turn leading back across the bridges you started on.

As you drive out of the campground after hiking the nature trail, look right (west) 100 yards from the trailhead to an atmospheric old road bridge. This is old US 441, since rerouted as the more modern Newfound Gap Road, now part of the Smokemont Loop Trail. If you'd like to see more of that route, it's easy to lengthen the nature trail walk a short distance by turning right (south) and following the informal trail mentioned above. You'll descend to that same old road, where a left (east) turn leads across the old bridge. Simply walk left (north) a short distance on the campground road to your car at the trailhead.

The stretch described above is part of the longer 6-mile hike beginning at the campground, the Smokemont Loop. Starting at the end of D loop, pass the gate on the gravel, road-width Bradley Fork Trail and reach the Chasteen Creek Trail on the right (north) at 1.2 miles.

Continue left (northwest) on the Bradley Fork Trail, then head left (west) at 1.7 miles on the Smokemont Loop Trail (the Bradley Fork Trail bears right/north). The Smokemont trail crosses a long, log footbridge, then makes a stiff 2-mile climb. Still climbing as it crosses to the west side of the ridge, the trail swings hard left (south) around one of the southernmost peaks of Richland Mountain. Dipping to a grassy little gap between summits (at about 3.5 miles), the trail starts its descent within earshot of Newfound Gap Road. Nearing the campground you might see Bradley Cemetery off to the right (south). Stay on the main trail and a little farther on, at about 5.4 miles, a side path leads back to the site, one of the largest cemeteries in the Smokies. Not far beyond, old US 441 leads into the campground. Walk back through the campground and at your car on D loop, it's a 6.1-mile hike.

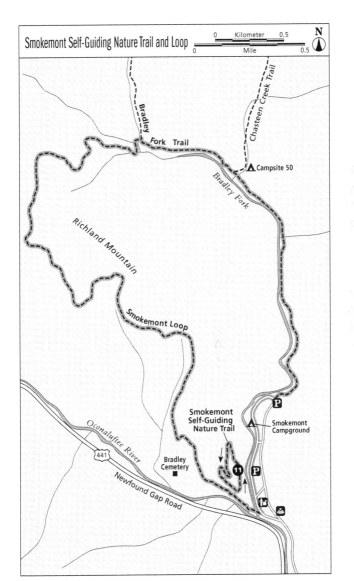

Smokemont Self-Guiding Nature Trail and Loop

Kilometer
0   0.5
Mile
0   0.5

N

Bradley
Fork   Trail

Chasteen Creek Trail

▲ Campsite 50

Bradley Fork

Richland Mountain

Smokemont Loop

Smokemont
Self-Guiding
Nature Trail

P

▲ Smokemont
   Campground

11

P

Oconaluftee River

441

Bradley
Cemetery ■

Newfound Gap Road

Miles and Directions

Smokemont Loop

0.0 Start at the D Loop trailhead on the Bradley Fork Trail.

1.2 Chasteen Creek Trail goes right (north); stay left (northwest) on Bradley Fork Trail.

1.7 Take the Smokemont Loop Trail to the left (west) and across the long bridge.

5.4 Arrive at Bradley Cemetery.

5.6 Return to the campground, then go left (north) to the end of D Loop.

6.1 Arrive back at the Bradley Fork trailhead.

Option

For an easy backpacking trip, start the Smokemont Loop hike as above, following the Bradley Fork Trail. Turn right (north) at 1.2 miles on the Chasteen Creek Trail and continue another 0.1 mile along the stream to campsite 50 (see above for reservation information). Start early and after setting up camp, Chasteen Creek Cascades is only 0.6 mile farther—the perfect afternoon day hike before dinner. Total round-trip: just 3.6 miles.

12 Ferguson Cabin

A best-kept secret, this national park entry point near the popular Maggie Valley resort area permits an easy hike to the highest historic log cabin in the Smokies.

Distance: 3.2-mile lollipop (or an optional 2.2-mile out and back to the cabin or an 8-mile out-and-back option to Hemphill Bald)

Hiking time: About 2 hours for the lollipop

Difficulty: Easy to moderate for the cabin, more challenging for Hemphill Bald

Trail surface: Gravel forest road, meadow path, and hardened forest trail

Other trail users: Some equestrian traffic near the Cataloochee Divide Trail

Best season: Spring through fall

Canine compatibility: Dogs not permitted

Fees and permits: Parking tag/ fee required if hiking more than 15 minutes (be sure to see Introduction)

Schedule: See "Special considerations" below

Maps: USGS Dellwood; TOPO! North Carolina, South Carolina

Trail contact: Appalachian Highlands Science Learning Center; (828) 926-6251

Special considerations: The environmental education center at Purchase Knob is a residence and research site for scientists and students studying the park and is not equipped to cater to drop-in visitors. Please park outside the gate (which still requires a parking tag) and do not block traffic or otherwise interfere with the facility's work. At times the center's staff may permit parking inside the gate until it's locked at 4:30; call the number above to check that option.

Finding the trailhead: From Asheville, North Carolina, go west on I-40. Take exit 20 and travel south on US 276 toward Maggie Valley. In 2.8 miles, turn right (west) onto Grindstone Road, then right (west) on Hemphill Road. Drive 3 miles. Pass the entrance to the Swag Country Inn on the left (west), and park 0.8 mile beyond near the gate for the Purchase Knob environmental education center. Please do not block the road or gate. From this trailhead, hike up the road to a meadow, where you'll see a directional sign to the cabin. GPS: N35 34 22.155' / W83 4 34.658'

The Hike

The circa-1870s John Love Ferguson Cabin, the Smokies' highest, sits 5,000 feet above sea level. It's easily accessible from the gate of the Appalachian Highlands Science Learning Center, one of the five such centers established in national parks in 2001. Once the estate of Voit Gilmore and Kathryn McNeil, the 530-acre tract surrounding the mountain Purchase Knob was donated to the park in 2000 and is the Smokies' largest private gift. The former summer home is now a facility where school and other groups come to help scientists in residence with park research.

A moderate lollipop loop starts at the learning center's gate. Walk up the scenic woods road and go left (west) across the meadow at a trail sign to Ferguson Cabin. Explore the inside. (*Option*: Backtrack to your car for a 2.2-mile hike.)

To continue the loop, exit the cabin and turn right (west) uphill into the woods along the stream. You'll cross the creek and reach a junction. To the west is a connector trail to the Cataloochee Divide Trail, but turn right (east) on the Ferguson Cabin Horse Trail to return to the meadow near the Ferguson Cabin sign. Turn right back to your car for a 3.2-miler.

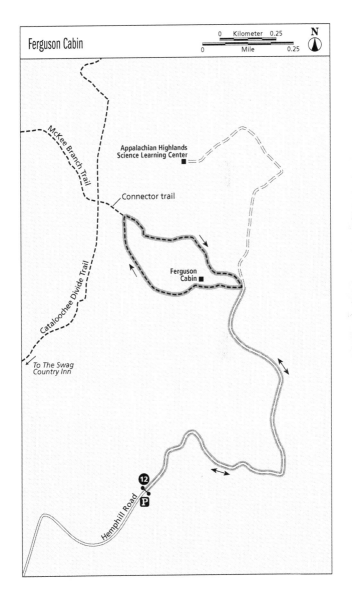

Ferguson Cabin

McKee Branch Trail

Appalachian Highlands
Science Learning Center

Connector trail

Cataloochee Divide Trail

Ferguson
Cabin

To The Swag
Country Inn

12

P

Hemphill Road

Kilometer

Mile

N

Miles and Directions

0.0 Start from the gate by hiking up the gravel road.

1.1 Reach the Ferguson Cabin.

2.1 Complete the loop from the meadow and cabin; turn right (south) on the road back to your car.

3.2 Arrive back at the trailhead.

Option

The Swag, a mile-high country inn you passed on your drive to Purchase Knob, is a favorite resort for hikers. Swag guests often visit Ferguson Cabin and nearby Hemphill Bald, a spectacular, hard-to-reach Smokies summit that is an easy hike from the inn. Extend the Ferguson cabin hike described here to Hemphill Bald with a left turn above the cabin, and another left on the Cataloochee Divide Trail. The Divide Trail passes the Swag to Double Gap, where the hike continues uphill on the Hemphill Bald Trail. Step out into the meadow about 4 miles from your car at a stone table sighting device (8 miles round-trip). From April through autumn, experts and naturalists engage Swag guests with interpretive programs and guided hikes. Next to the inn's lodge, with its national reputation for fine food and lodging, a hollow tree trunk holds hiking staffs. A wooden medallion with a guest's name hangs from every staff, inviting them to grab theirs and stride off on a hike. A stay in one of the inn's ancient Appalachian log cabin cottages is a magical experience (theswag.com).

13 The Boogerman Trail

This hike mixes multiple bridge crossings on Caldwell Fork Trail, one of the Smokies' best stream hikes, with historic ruins and sights of the Smokies' inspiring ancient forests along the Boogerman Trail.

Distance: 7.6-mile loop (with options for out-and-back hikes and a 9.6-mile backpacking trip)

Hiking time: About 5 hours

Difficulty: Moderate for the loop, easy for an out-and-back trek. More challenging for backpacking, mostly due to distance and possible muck.

Trail surface: Typical forest path for Boogerman. Mixed horse/hiker use on the Caldwell Fork Trail makes for some mud and rocks.

Other trail users: Horses are permitted on the Caldwell Fork Trail.

Best season: Drier weather periods in winter and fall

Canine compatibility: Dogs not permitted

Fees and permits: Parking tag/fee required if hiking more than 15 minutes (be sure to see Introduction)

Schedule: Heavy snow might complicate access on the Cataloochee area's unpaved roads.

Maps: USGS Cove Creek Gap and Dellwood; TOPO! North Carolina, South Carolina

Trail contacts: Information about trails, camping, road closures, as well as downloadable maps and a "Smokies Trip Planner" is available online under the "Plan Your Visit" part of the park's excellent website, www.nps.gov/grsm. Since 2013 backcountry campers have been required to have reservations and a permit for all overnight camping in the park (a fee is charged). The Smokies is a very popular backpacking destination, so the park's regulations are extensive, and policies differ for General Backcountry Permits and AT Thru-Hiker Permits. If you want to reserve campsite 41, visit the park's permit and reservation website for further information and to process your permit (https://smokiespermits.nps.gov). The park recommends calling the Backcountry Information Office as the preferred way to clarify camping regulations and ask trip-planning questions; open 8 a.m. to 5 p.m. daily, (865) 436-1297.

Special considerations: Since the last edition of this book, significant floods have claimed many of the bridges along the Caldwell Fork Trail. It is safe to say that the resulting rock-hop stream crossings will be drier and easier in the driest weather. A hiking staff or trekking poles and higher-top boots might also make it easier to navigate the muddy spots found on this horse-friendly trail.

Finding the trailhead: From Asheville, North Carolina, take I-40 to exit 20, and go south toward Maggie Valley on US 276. Take the first right on Cove Creek Road, heading north, and go 7.4 miles to a left turn, on the road to Cataloochee, where the road changes from gravel to pavement. The Caldwell Fork Trail begins on the left (south) in 3.1 miles at a small roadside pullout just beyond the Cataloochee Campground (where restrooms are available in season). GPS: N35 37 53.504' / W83 05.283'

The Hike

The Caldwell Fork Trail bisects a huge drainage, where a variety of trails create diverse day and overnight circuit hikes. A 7.4-mile loop using the Boogerman Trail is one of the best. Leave the tiny parking spot beside the road on Caldwell Fork Trail, and cross a big single log bridge, the first of twenty that lead up this trail. This may be your first photo—it's a great downstream nature shot, not to mention with one of your hiking companions standing on the bridge! (At press time, the park was advising that water crossings on Caldwell Fork Trail might require wading. Call the Backcountry Information Office, 865-436-1297, for the latest conditions.)

At 0.8 mile head left (southeast) on the Boogerman Trail. It winds away and above the Caldwell Fork, eventually

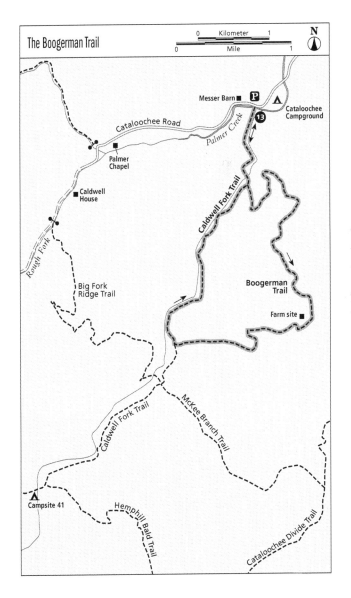

The Boogerman Trail

Kilometer
0   1
Mile
0   1

N

Messer Barn   P

Cataloochee Campground

Cataloochee Road

Palmer Creek

13

Palmer Chapel

Caldwell House

Rough Fork

Big Fork Ridge Trail

Caldwell Fork Trail

Boogerman Trail

Farm site

Caldwell Fork Trail

McKee Branch Trail

Campsite 41

Hemphill Bald Trail

Cataloochee Divide Trail

returning at 4.9 miles after rising along the west flank of the prominent Cataloochee Divide. Along the way you'll cross small bridges and easily hop streams on a refreshingly "hikers only" path that undulates through tall timber, the result of Robert "Booger" Palmer's refusal to cut the big trees on his stream-laced property. You'll pass through "Booger's" farm site; be on the lookout later for an especially impressive stone wall and then others, not so well preserved. As you near Caldwell Fork Trail look left (south) for the last remnants of Carson Messer's cabin. Turn right (north), traveling back along Caldwell Fork to your car.

Miles and Directions

0.0 Start by crossing the long log bridge on the Caldwell Fork Trail.

0.8 Turn left (southeast) from the Caldwell Fork Trail onto the Boogerman Trail.

4.9 Turn right (north) on the Caldwell Fork Trail.

6.8 Pass the first Boogerman Trail junction.

7.6 Arrive back at the trailhead.

Options

The easiest hike in this area is a simple out-and-back on the Caldwell Fork Trail. As Boogerman hikers discover, views are awesome along the stream—and from the bridges. Just turn around when you want.

If the weather's dry and horse traffic hasn't made the trail too muddy, backpackers can make an easy overnighter out of this gradual streamside walk to the Smokies' designated campsite 41, 4.8 miles south on Caldwell Fork Trail from the parking area. Along the Caldwell Fork Trail you pass both entrances to the Boogerman Trail (on the left/east), the Big Fork Ridge Trail at 3.2 miles (on the right/

northwest), the McKee Branch Trail at 3.3 miles on the left/ southeast (site of the Caldwell Fork community and its grist mill), and Hemphill Bald Trail on the left (southeast) at 4.7 miles. Cross the final bridge over Caldwell Fork to reach campsite 41. Take a rest, but consider going a ways beyond the campsite. A side trail to the right (north) soon leads you to "Big Poplars," a grove of towering, centuries-old tulip poplars. These awesome giants were spared by Cataloochee resident John Caldwell. Above that, the hardwood and hemlock forest becomes impressively mature. Backtrack for an approximately 10-mile overnighter.

14 Big Creek

A waterfall, wading spots, and a scenic backcountry campsite make this a temptingly multifaceted day or overnight hike.

Distance: 4 miles out and back to the waterfall; an out-and-back backpack option of 10.6 miles

Hiking time: 2–3 hours to Mouse Creek Falls and back

Difficulty: Moderate, more challenging if you backpack to the campsite

Trail surface: Gradual old railroad grade

Other trail users: Equestrians, but it's easy to avoid evidence of their "passing"

Best season: Year-round

Canine compatibility: Dogs not permitted

Fees and permits: Parking tag/fee required if hiking more than 15 minutes (be sure to see Introduction)

Schedule: Heavy snow might complicate access on the Deep Creek area's unpaved roads.

Maps: USGS Waterville, Cove Creek Gap, Luftee Knob; TOPO! North Carolina, South Carolina

Trail contacts: Information about trails, camping, road closures, as well as downloadable maps and a "Smokies Trip Planner" is available online under the "Plan Your Visit" part of the park's excellent website, www.nps.gov/grsm. Since 2013, backcountry campers have been required to have reservations and a permit for all overnight camping in the park (a fee is charged). The Smokies is a very popular backpacking destination, so the park's regulations are extensive, and policies differ for General Backcountry Permits and AT Thru-Hiker Permits. If you want to reserve campsite 37, visit the park's permit and reservation website for further information and to process your permit (https://smokiespermits.nps.gov). The park recommends calling the Backcountry Information Office as the preferred way to clarify camping regulations and ask trip-planning questions; open 8 a.m. to 5 p.m. daily, (865) 436-1297.

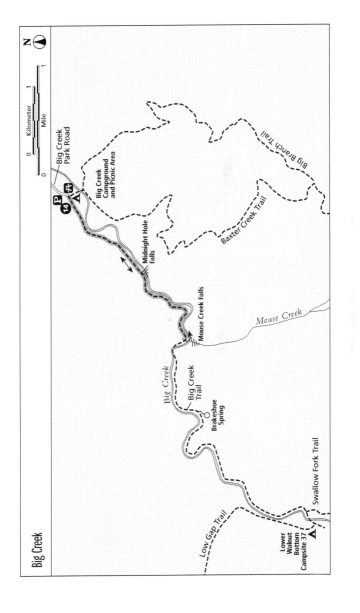

Big Creek

N

Big Creek Park Road

Big Creek Campground and Picnic Area

Midnight Hole Falls

Baxter Creek Trail

Big Branch Trail

Mouse Creek Falls

Mouse Creek

Big Creek

Big Creek Trail

Brakeshoe Spring

Low Gap Trail

Lower Walnut Bottom Campsite 37

Swallow Fork Trail

Kilometer

Mile

Finding the trailhead: From I-40 near the Tennessee/North Carolina state line, take exit 451 (in Tennessee) for Waterville. Turn back under the interstate to turn left across the Pigeon River and left again on Waterville Road. Two miles from the interstate come to a crossroads in the village of Mount Sterling. Follow the sign straight through the intersection onto a gravel road; the Big Creek Ranger Station is 0.2 mile ahead on the right (west). Pass the Ranger Station, the horse use area sign, and the Big Creek trailhead sign to park in the lot beyond (where restrooms are available). GPS: N35 45 06.793' / W83 06.583'

The Hike

Take off up the old logging railroad grade, nicely rehabbed in spring 2022 by the Trails Forever program. It bumps up abruptly at first, then rises its entire length along Big Creek, one of the park's most scenic streams. The grade lies on the right (north) side of Big Creek on this lower section of the trail. At 1.4 miles, Midnight Hole is a deep pool at the base of a ledge cascade.

Go left at 2.0 miles on a side trail to see Mouse Creek Falls as it cascades spectacularly into Big Creek on the opposite side of the stream. Retrace your steps to complete the gradual 4-mile round-trip day hike.

Miles and Directions

0.0 Start by following the old railroad grade along Big Creek.

1.4 Arrive at Midnight Hole.

2.0 Reach Mouse Creek Falls.

4.0 Turn around to retrace your steps back to the trailhead.

Option

To make this a backpacking trip, continue on the Big Creek Trail beyond Mouse Creek Falls. Just above the falls, a bridge crosses to the left, or southeast side, of the creek.

At just less than 3 miles, Brakeshoe Spring is on the left (south), named during logging railroad days when a brake shoe was placed under the rivulet to catch water. The creek winds more sharply above the spring, and the Swallow Fork Trail goes left (south) at 5.1 miles. The Big Creek Trail crosses the creek for the last time to the Lower Walnut Bottom backcountry campsite 37, at 5.3 miles.

Backpackers would do well to consider this campsite. It's a very scenic setting, and the hike is only a 10.6-mile round-trip, with an elevation gain of 1,000 feet (also doable for more energetic day hikers). This is a popular campsite, in part because it accommodates 20 backpackers but not horse campers.

Additional Miles and Directions

Continuing westward from Mouse Creek Falls, the turnaround point for the day hike:

2.8 Pass Brakeshoe Spring on the left (south).

5.1 Swallow Fork Trail goes left (south); stay straight to the campsite.

5.3 Arrive at campsite 37. Spend the night, then return as you came.

10.6 Arrive back at the trailhead.

Southwest Section

15 Spruce-Fir Self-Guiding Nature Trail

This short nature trail wanders what was once a Canadian zone forest of whispering evergreens. The trail and its interpretive brochure showcase the environmental factors that are killing trees in many of the world's high-elevation woodlands.

Distance: 0.4-mile lollipop loop that can be hiked in either direction

Hiking time: About 30 minutes

Difficulty: Easy

Trail surface: Smooth forest floor and plank bog bridges across low spots where water pools in wet weather

Other trail users: None; no bikes or horses allowed

Best season: Summer for lushness; winter for stark landscapes

Canine compatibility: Dogs not permitted

Fees and permits: Parking tag/fee required if hiking more than 15 minutes (be sure to see Introduction)

Schedule: The Clingmans Dome Road is closed in winter Dec 1 through Mar 31 (when cross-country skiers, snowshoers, and winter walkers rule the road).

Maps: USGS Clingmans Dome; TOPO! North Carolina, South Carolina

Trail contacts: Information about trails, camping, road closures, as well as downloadable maps and a "Smokies Trip Planner" is available online under the "Plan Your Visit" part of the park's excellent website, www.nps.gov/grsm.

Special considerations: An interpretive brochure is available at the trailhead. It's safest and easiest to pull into this tiny trailhead going east on the way back from your visit to Clingmans Dome (restrooms available).

Other: If you reach the Smokies from the Blue Ridge Parkway, notice the interpretive information about forest decline evident at Mount Mitchell and Richland Balsam, both featured in FalconGuides' *Best Easy Day Hikes Blue Ridge Parkway*.

Finding the trailhead: The Spruce-Fir Self-Guiding Nature Trail is on the Clingmans Dome Road, 2.6 miles from the junction with Newfound Gap Road, 18.4 miles from the Oconaluftee Visitor Center, and 15.8 miles from the Sugarlands Visitor Center. GPS: N35 35 741' / W83 27.519'

The Hike

Early on, it was known that the Fraser fir in this high forest was being decimated by the balsam woolly adelgid, a pest introduced into the United States around 1900. But that didn't explain the decline of the red spruces that also grow here. More recent studies suggest damage to both species by acid rain—highly acidic precipitation that upsets the pH balance of the soil, freeing heavy metals that inhibit a tree's ability to ingest nutrients. Another significant factor has been discovered: ozone. Research suggests that, like the smog trapped in cities, airborne pollution from major utilities and industries located upwind leads to startlingly high ozone levels on southern summits. Such pollution, often contained in cloud caps as acidic as vinegar, burns the needles of firs, dramatically inhibiting the growth and survival of evergreens already fighting a severe climate. The result is that stark tree skeletons stand here and elsewhere in the park, tall and gray in ghostlike groves. Luckily, early 1990s changes to the Clean Air Act seem to be helping a little.

Another of the natural forces challenging these high elevation forests is wind. When openings appear as weakened trees fall, healthier trees suffer the fuller force of the wind. On one side of this loop, you'll see a spruce that fell despite a huge root system.

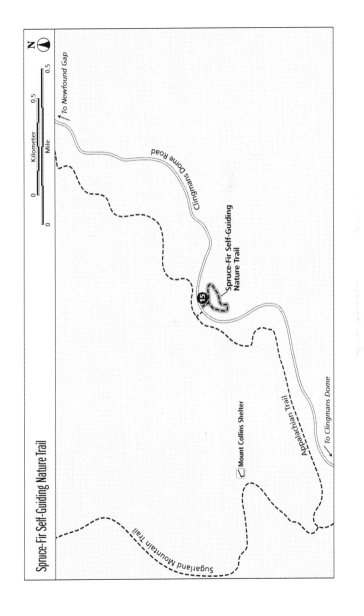

Spruce-Fir Self-Guiding Nature Trail

Kilometer
0   0.5

Mile
0   0.5

N

To Newfound Gap

Clingmans Dome Road

Spruce-Fir Self-Guiding
Nature Trail

15

Mount Collins Shelter

Appalachian Trail

To Clingmans Dome

Sugarland Mountain Trail

The taller trees may be dying, but you'll see younger trees springing up before suffering themselves. Beyond appreciating the decline of this forest, use your time on this trail to notice many other spruce-fir forest species of plants, animals, and birds, but watch your step. You won't want to divert your eyes too long from the almost continuous "bog log" walkway you'll traverse through this damp, high elevation area. Even that elevated treadway adds to the northern feel of this trail.

The ultimate irony may be that even as we argue the causes of global warming, these boreal forests, so dependent for survival on the South's coldest climate, are being challenged by simple air pollution. That same pollution can make hiking a little harder on hazy days, and the park indeed issues pollution alerts. There's no better place in the Smokies to experience the unfolding tragedy of what we're doing to our planet.

16 Clingmans Dome

The Smokies'—and Tennessee's—highest peak (6,643 feet) is more than just another chance to add to your life list of grandiose summits to conquer. The vista is astounding when the weather's right.

Distance: 1 mile out and back
Hiking time: About 1.5 hours
Difficulty: Moderate for trail surface, but it is steep. Just take your time.
Trail surface: Paved
Other trail users: None
Best season: Nov is the clearest nonwinter month.
Canine compatibility: Dogs not permitted
Fees and permits: Parking tag/fee required if hiking more than 15 minutes (be sure to see Introduction)

Schedule: The Clingmans Dome Road is closed in winter Dec 1 through Mar 31.
Maps: USGS Clingmans Dome; TOPO! Tennessee, Kentucky
Trail contacts: Information about trails, camping, road closures, as well as downloadable maps and a "Smokies Trip Planner" is available online under the "Plan Your Visit" part of the park's excellent website, www.nps.gov/grsm.
Special considerations: Get going early on this hike; the parking lot will be emptier.

Finding the trailhead: The Clingmans Dome parking area is on the Clingmans Dome Road, 7.6 miles west of the junction with Newfound Gap Road. Restrooms are in the parking lot. GPS: N35 33.389' / W83 29.721'

The Hike

Grab that restroom break, then take the steep paved path past rest benches. You'll pass a connector to the AT on the left (north), then reach and ascend the tower path that

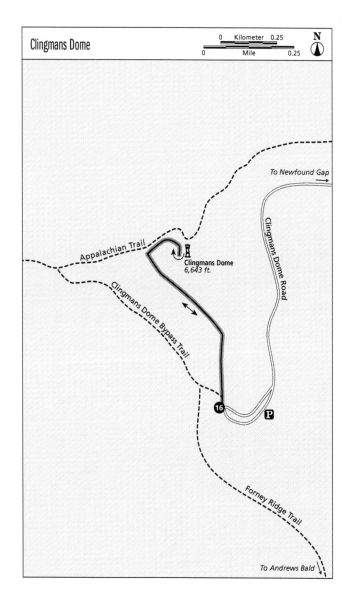

Clingmans Dome

To Newfound Gap

Appalachian Trail

Clingmans Dome Road

Clingmans Dome
6,643 ft.

Clingmans Dome Bypass Trail

16

P

Forney Ridge Trail

To Andrews Bald

N

0   Kilometer   0.25

0   Mile   0.25

corkscrews its way above the peak. The increasingly thinned evergreen forest here (take the Spruce-Fir Nature Trail to learn more about the park's ecological issues) affords even better views than when a tower was first needed to reach above the trees.

Winter offers the best views from Clingmans Dome, but the road is closed December to March due to predictably heavy snowfalls. Only cross-country skiers willing to ski 14 miles round-trip (or winter backpackers on the AT) are likely to see the broad curve of the Earth from the tower.

Nevertheless, the high southern Appalachians routinely receive summer cold-front incursions that redeem the mountains' reputation for the region's coolest summer weather. Use your clearest day for this hike—or not. There is something to be said for exploring the inside of a cloud at nearly 7,000 feet. You'll remember the damp, cool, dripping realm of Clingmans Dome even if you can't see down to Cherokee.

Miles and Directions

0.0   Start in the parking lot.

0.5   Follow the path to reach the top of Clingmans Dome.

1.0   Arrive back at the trailhead.

17 Juney Whank Falls

This is a nice mini-waterfall walk for kids and those with only a little time.

Distance: 0.7-mile loop

Hiking time: 1 hour

Difficulty: Moderate, for its climb and steeper descent

Trail surface: Mostly road grade or packed trail

Other trail users: You may see equestrians along the bridle trail portion of this hike.

Best season: Best in spring or after a rain, which increases the flow in this small stream.

Canine compatibility: Dogs not permitted

Fees and permits: Parking tag/fee required if hiking more than 15 minutes (be sure to see Introduction)

Schedule: Year-round

Maps: USGS Bryson City; TOPO! North Carolina, South Carolina

Trail contacts: Information about trails, camping, road closures, as well as downloadable maps and a "Smokies Trip Planner" is available online under the "Plan Your Visit" part of the park's excellent website, www.nps.gov/grsm.

Special considerations: You won't need to cope with a busy parking area if you camp at Deep Creek Campground (especially at campsites 30 and up), where it's easy to step up onto Galbraith Creek Road. Go left (northwest) across the bridge, and you can hike both to Juney Whank Falls and on the Deep Creek Loop.

Finding the trailhead: Take well-signed routes north from downtown Bryson City into the park. After passing the cluster of businesses at the park boundary, pass the Deep Creek Campground and the picnic area (where restrooms are available in season), both on the right (east), and turn left into the parking area as you reach a bridge on the right (east) (the Galbraith Creek Road). The road ahead is a circular drop-off point. Take the gravel grade at the upper left (north) end of the lot. GPS: N35 27.854' / W83 26.064'

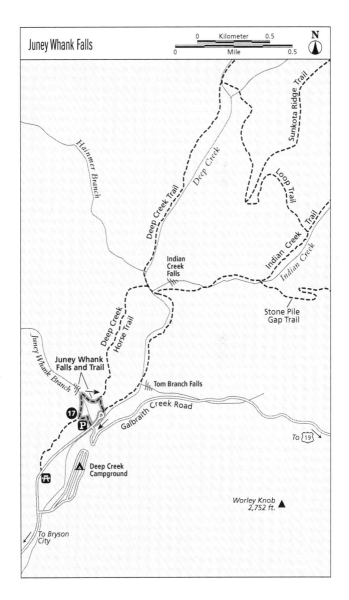

Juney Whank Falls

Hainmer Branch

Deep Creek Trail

Deep Creek

Sunkota Ridge Trail

Loop Trail

Indian Creek Trail

Indian Creek

Indian Creek Falls

Stone Pile Gap Trail

Deep Creek Horse Trail

Juney Whank Branch

Juney Whank Falls and Trail

Tom Branch Falls

17

P

Galbraith Creek Road

To 19

Deep Creek Campground

Worley Knob 2,752 ft.

To Bryson City

Kilometer   0   0.5
Mile   0   0.5

N

The Hike

Climb the wide road grade up and left (north) from the parking lot to a junction with the Deep Creek Horse Trail. The bridle trail descends left and rises right: Turn right (south) up the wood steps, and shortly turn right again (northeast) at the "Falls" sign. The trail dips down nice rock steps and crosses a scenic bridge below the falls, where you'll find an embedded bench. Just past the bridge, there's a perfect rock seat at the base of the falls. You could almost picture a Romantic poet perched there pondering. Near the falls, "This Is Not a Trail" signs are actually embedded in some bootleg paths that might mislead the inexperienced.

The trail rises beyond the falls and rejoins the bridle trail that crossed the stream above the cascade. Turn right (east) at the bridle trail junction beyond the falls. This area is very well signed and easy to follow. Just ahead, turn right (southeast) again off the bridle trail at another sign and descend a steep, mountain laurel-sheltered gully. Don't fear—what once was a steep ditch has been wonderfully tamed. A raised graveled tread with steps on the left isolates a rainfall course on the right, with water breaks to foil erosion. If you're not a trail expert, be aware this is an artful solution to an otherwise erosion-prone piece of path!

At the bottom—and more signs—turn right (southwest) on the Deep Creek Trail, and head back to the parking lot.

Miles and Directions

0.0 Start on the road grade.

0.1 Reach the bridle trail junction and go up the wood steps.

0.3 Arrive at Juney Whank Falls.

0.7 Arrive back at the trailhead.

18 Deep Creek Loop

This truly great, longer circuit hike starts with what may be the park's easiest (no doubt accessible) walk to a spectacular waterfall, Toms Branch Falls, not to mention Indian Creek Falls.

Distance: 4.4-mile lollipop with 1.6 and 3.4-mile out-and-back options

Hiking time: 1–2 hours to the waterfalls and return, 2–3 hours for the loop

Difficulty: Easy (for Tom Branch Falls) to moderate for Indian Creek Falls and back, and more challenging for the entire loop hike

Trail surface: Gravel road grades with stable footing and firm, packed-soil forest trails

Other trail users: You may see equestrians along portions of this hike. Some trail users may be swimsuit-wearing, tube-toting float trippers on the lowest section of Deep Creek (the park discourages water recreation, but it's permitted at this one spot). Mountain bikers are permitted to ride to the upper stream bridge on the Deep Creek Trail.

Best season: After a rain for the waterfalls; in the off-season for more solitude in this popular multiuse area

Canine compatibility: Dogs are not permitted.

Fees and permits: Parking tag/fee required if hiking more than 15 minutes (be sure to see Introduction)

Schedule: Year-round

Maps: USGS Bryson City; TOPO! North Carolina, South Carolina

Trail contacts: Information about trails, camping, road closures, as well as downloadable maps and a "Smokies Trip Planner" is available online under the "Plan Your Visit" part of the park's excellent website, www.nps.gov/grsm. Since 2013, backcountry campers have been required to have advance reservations and a permit for all overnight camping in the park (a fee is charged). The Smokies is a very popular backpacking destination, so the park's regulations are extensive and policies differ for General Back-country Permits and AT Thru-Hiker Permits. If you want to reserve campsite 60, visit the park's permit and reservation website for further information and to process your permit (https://smokiespermits.nps.gov). The park recommends calling the Backcountry Information Office as the preferred way to clarify camping regulations and ask trip-planning questions; open 8 a.m. to 5 p.m. daily, (865) 436-1297. **Special considerations:** You won't have to cope with a busy parking area if you camp at Deep Creek Campground (especially at campsites 30 and up), where it's easy to step up onto Galbraith Creek Road. Go left (northwest) across the bridge, and take the trail to the right (north).

Finding the trailhead: Take well-signed routes north from down-town Bryson City into the park. After passing the cluster of businesses at the park boundary, pass the Deep Creek Campground and the picnic area, both on the right (east), and turn left (northeast) into the parking area. A bridge is on the right (east) (Galbraith Creek Road). The road ahead (northeast) is a circular drop-off point. A restroom is available year-round at a picnic pavilion on the left before the trail-head. GPS: N35 27.854' / W83 26.064'

The Hike

Just driving into the Deep Creek area conveys an important Smokies' impression—these summits may not tower like the Tetons, but you sense that there's a vast wildland ahead that stretches ridge after ridge beyond the park boundary. This hike takes you a ways into that forest.

Head off up the level road grade along the wide, green, and pristine Deep Creek as it flows from the heart of the Smokies. Soon, the sound of the stream rises to a higher pitch and as you amble up to five benches on the riverside . . . there's awesome Tom Branch Falls plummeting into the water on the opposite side of Deep Creek. The road continues along the stream past more benches and then turns right (east) to cross a bridge. There's a great view above the bridge and from benches across the stream where the road surges more steeply above the creek. At 0.7 mile, the Indian Creek Trail veers right (east) from the Deep Creek Trail at a sign prohibiting tubing above that point.

Go right (east) on the Indian Creek Trail, and in just a few hundred feet, a side trail descends left (north) to scenic Indian Creek Falls (a 1.6-mile round-trip from the parking area). Continuing on the Indian Creek Trail across another bridge, you'll pass Stone Pile Gap Trail as it drops right (southeast) at 1.2 miles. Beyond, the road grade rises with the river above rhododendron-covered stream banks into a drier forest. Turn left (northwest) on the Loop Trail at 1.5 miles. After a level stretch the trail rises steeply up and left (south) to crest at the Sunkota Ridge Trail at 2.0 miles. If anything, the trail drops more steeply off the other side. As you pass a massive white oak, the sound of Deep Creek comes from below.

The trail levels and rejoins the Deep Creek Trail at a T junction at 2.7 miles. To the right (north), the old logging railroad grade appears trail-like on its way to scenic campsite 60 (a gradual, graded 5.2-mile round-trip from the trailhead on the Deep Creek Trail for an easy backpack). You will need a reservation to use campsite 60. Turning left (southwest), the gravel road crosses a bridge (the upper limit of mountain bike access). Below a little rapid, a pool in Deep Creek must be 15 feet deep.

The trail drops steeply at only one point on its way to another bridge and back to the Indian Creek Trail junction at 3.7 miles. From the junction it's another 0.7 mile back to your car for a 4.4-mile hike.

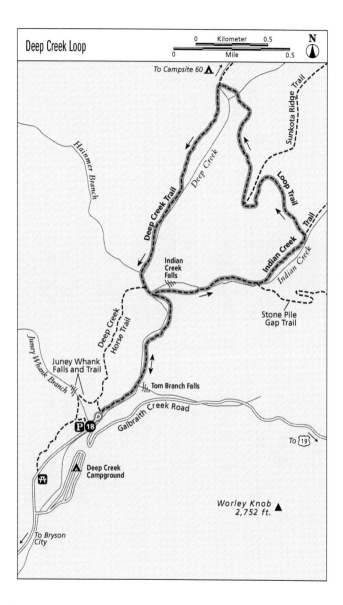

Deep Creek Loop

Kilometer
0   0.5
0   0.5
Mile

N

To Campsite 60 ▲

Sunkota Ridge Trail

Deep Creek

Deep Creek Trail

Hammer Branch

Loop Trail

Indian Creek Trail

Indian
Creek
Falls

Indian Creek

Deep Creek Horse Trail

Stone Pile
Gap Trail

Juney Whank Branch

Juney Whank
Falls and Trail

Tom Branch Falls

P 18

Galbraith Creek Road

To 19

Deep Creek
Campground

To Bryson
City

Worley Knob ▲
2,752 ft.

Miles and Directions

0.0 Start by heading up the Deep Creek Trail.

0.2 Reach Tom Branch Falls.

0.7 Reach the junction with the Indian Creek Trail and go right (east).

1.5 Go left (northwest) on the Loop Trail.

2.7 Turn left (southwest), heading back on the Deep Creek Trail.

3.7 Pass the Indian Creek Trail junction.

4.4 Arrive back at the trailhead.

Option

The Deep Creek Trail, from the trailhead to the upper bridge, is 3.4 miles out and back with only one steep stretch.

Northwest Section

19 Cove Hardwoods Nature Trail

Here you'll find one of the park's best places to savor the towering grandeur of the old-growth cove hardwood forests that were so characteristic of the virgin Smokies. This must-see trail is the essential Smokies, in one short, inspiring hike.

Distance: 1-mile lollipop
Hiking time: About 1 hour
Difficulty: Easy to moderate
Trail surface: Even forest path with paved steeper sections
Other trail users: None; no dogs or horses allowed
Best season: April's great for carpets of spring flowers and views to the still leafless tops of soaring trees. Summer is best for the deep shade of a cathedral grove.
Canine compatibility: Dogs not permitted
Fees and permits: Parking tag/fee required if hiking more than 15 minutes (be sure to see Introduction)

Schedule: Closed only when inclement weather closes Newfound Gap Road
Maps: USGS Mount Le Conte; TOPO! Tennessee, Kentucky
Trail contacts: Information about trails, camping, road closures, as well as downloadable maps and a "Smokies Trip Planner" is available online under the "Plan Your Visit" part of the park's excellent website, www.nps.gov/grsm.
Special considerations: The self-guiding brochure for this trail is particularly worth purchasing—it's available at the trailhead dispenser and at the park's visitor centers.

Finding the trailhead: From Newfound Gap Road turn east into the Chimneys Picnic Area, located 8.6 miles north of Newfound Gap and 4.6 miles south of the Sugarlands Visitor Center. Pull into the first parking slip on the right (south), below the trailhead sign and steps. The picnic area's first picturesque stone restroom is to the left and just downhill. GPS: N35 38.193' / W83 29.529'

The Hike

The Chimneys Picnic Area and this nature trail serve up the "forest primeval" of stereotype. Not every unlogged forest appears "virgin" in the towering way found here. This perfect ecosystem of heavy rain and deep, rich soils permits deciduous species such as beech, yellow buckeye, red maple, basswood, yellow birch, and coniferous hemlocks to reach record proportions of grandeur in height, circumference, and age (as old as 500 years).

From the trailhead, up the timber-framed steps past a group picnic site, the trail splits: Take a right. The trail rises to the east above the sounds of Newfound Gap Road. Near post #5 there's a huge, old hemlock felled beside the trail, with its annual rings ripe for counting. The timber-boxed steps continue as you rise into a broad cove at 0.25 mile, then into a drainage. Swing back and forth across a stream on old-fashioned stone and concrete bridging from an earlier era. The open understory is nothing but wildflowers.

The trail leads left (southwest) of the stream, and more directly up the cove from former fields and a smaller, selectively harvested forest into old growth. After a long stretch of old concrete tread near post #9, at about 0.3 mile, the trees rise to appear much like the climax forest that so impressed the earliest Appalachian explorers—and was later almost eradicated by early twentieth-century logging companies.

At post #12, you could pinch a nerve in your neck trying to see the very tops of these trees. You'd need a family of tree huggers to express affection for this one, a yellow buckeye, one of the biggest at more than 12 feet in diameter. This is the top of the loop. If you look uphill, you can imagine the towering trees marching upward for miles—and they once

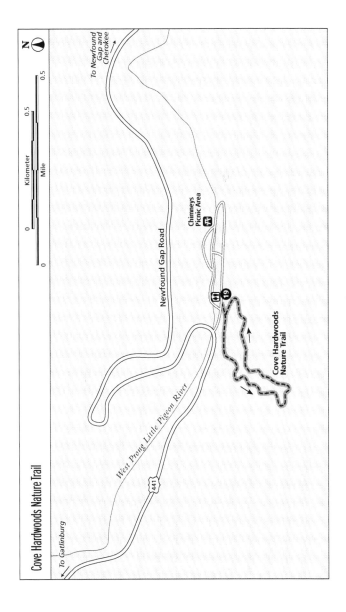

Cove Hardwoods Nature Trail

did throughout the Smokies. The widely spaced trees dominate their patch of soil and reach for every ray of sunlight available. An open, uncluttered, parklike setting lies below.

The trail dips steeply from here into a drier forest, past benches, on a graveled, rocky path. The trail eventually veers right, out of the drainage, at about 0.5 mile, just above your earlier trail and back to the closing of the loop and the picnic area.

Many places in the southern Appalachians once sheltered impressive stands such as these. Today, those that remain are few and far between. This is one of the most accessible. Elsewhere in the Smokies, consider hiking the Cosby Self-Guiding Nature Trail if you're in the northeast part of the park. If a future trip takes you to Nantahala National Forest in western North Carolina, the Joyce Kilmer Memorial Forest is another such forest trail (see FalconGuides' *Hiking North Carolina*).

Miles and Directions

0.0 Start by heading up the timber-framed steps.

0.2 Travel on an old-style concrete path amid streams and wildflowers.

0.4 Reach the top of the loop amid towering trees.

1.0 Arrive back at the trailhead.

20 Chimney Tops Trail

This is still one of the Smokies' true peak experiences, even though the 2016 Chimney Tops 2 fire closed the uppermost part of the trail. There are still great views from a newly constructed viewpoint just below the exhilarating exposure found at the top of this rocky summit. There's also a side trip on the Road Prong Trail that follows the remnants of the park's oldest Native American trail and first transmountain road as it rises toward the peaks.

Distance: About 3.5 miles out and back (4 miles out and back if and when the park ever reopens the summit); plus up to 6.6 miles out and back on Road Prong options

Hiking time: 2–3 hours

Difficulty: More challenging, this hike rises almost 1,500 vertical feet.

Trail surface: Road-width and rocky

Other trail users: None; no dogs or horses allowed

Best season: Spring, when the peak stands above lower lime-green mountainsides, and late fall. Winter can create tricky footing.

Canine compatibility: Dogs not permitted

Fees and permits: Parking tag/fee required if hiking more than 15 minutes (be sure to see Introduction)

Schedule: The once adventurous rock climb to the very top of the summit is closed due to the Chimney Tops 2 Fire. The trail itself is closed only when inclement weather closes Newfound Gap Road.

Maps: USGS Mount Le Conte; TOPO! Tennessee, Kentucky

Trail contacts: Information about trails, camping, road closures, as well as downloadable maps and a "Smokies Trip Planner" is available online under the "Plan Your Visit" part of the park's excellent website, www.nps.gov/grsm. The park recommends calling the Back-country Information Office as the preferred way to clarify camping regulations and ask trip-planning questions; open 8 a.m. to 5 p.m. daily, (865) 436-1297.

Special considerations: This is one of the hikes in this book that is not easy, indeed it is "more challenging," but it was selected because it's one of the shortest high-adventure hikes. Do not undertake this trail lightly, but it is often hiked by well-equipped, motivated novices in good shape. That, of course, makes this an extremely popular path. Go very early, during the week, and in the off-season to be sure parking is available and to avoid passing lanes on the trail! You can't miss the inspiring stone stairways built on this trail in 2012 by the Trails Forever program.

Finding the trailhead: The Chimney Tops parking area is on Newfound Gap Road, 7.1 miles south of the Sugarlands Visitor Center, 2.5 miles south of the Chimneys Picnic Area (closest available restrooms), and 22 miles north of the Oconaluftee Visitor Center. GPS: N35 38.146' / W83 28.195'

The Hike

This popular trail launches as a wide and graded path down to a bridge over Walker Camp Prong. It's uphill from there, and not far beyond you'll cross another bridge, this time over Road Prong. Together, these streams scour the valley below as the West Prong of the Little Pigeon River.

The trail ascends along gushing Road Prong. After the third bridge on that stream, head right (west) at the junction, where the Road Prong Trail continues left (south) up the watershed (described in the option below). Not far above the turn, the trail stands steeply up, confined in a tight ramp toward the ridge crest of Sugarland Mountain. As the trail veers right (north), the grade becomes more gradual, then reaches the apex of the ridge that leads to where the Chimneys rise into the sky.

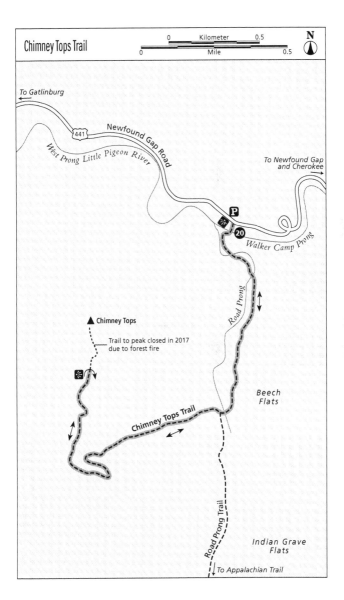

Chimney Tops Trail

Kilometer
0   0.5
Mile
0   0.5

N

To Gatlinburg

441 Newfound Gap Road

West Prong Little Pigeon River

To Newfound Gap
and Cherokee

P

20 Walker Camp Prong

Road Prong

▲ Chimney Tops

Trail to peak closed in 2017
due to forest fire

Beech
Flats

Chimney Tops Trail

Indian Grave
Flats

Road Prong Trail

To Appalachian Trail

The viewpoint from where the trail has ended since 2017 is a nice turnaround despite missing what was once the final climb, a rocky, low-grade rock climb up the crags.

Savor the vista. To the northwest, the Sugarlands Valley plummets to Gatlinburg. Northeast, the squiggle of The Loop in the Newfound Gap Road lies below. Far above, Mount LeConte shows off all four of its named summits.

Miles and Directions

0.0 Start from the parking area.

0.1 Cross the first bridge over Walker Camp Prong.

0.4 Cross the second bridge over Road Prong.

0.8 Cross the third bridge over Road Prong.

0.9 At the Road Prong Trail junction, stay right (west) on the Chimney Tops Trail.

1.75 Reach the turnaround point below the Chimney Tops summit. Until the summit reopens, enjoy the view at the high point currently open.

3.5 Arrive back at the trailhead (expected to be about 4 miles when the summit reopens).

Option

If you'd like to see a lofty, more defined section of the old road across the Smokies like the Sugarlands Valley Self-Guiding Nature Trail, follow the Chimney Tops Trail for 0.9 mile, and where that trail turns right (west), follow the Road Prong Trail left (south) as far as you care to walk. This historic old Native American trail, said to be the oldest in the park, has seen centuries of travel on its rise to and across Indian Gap.

The trail was upgraded to road status in the 1830s and was the only road over the Smokies until the 1920s, when the Newfound Gap Road was built. Indian Gap was once thought to be the Smokies' lowest gap, until Professor Arnold Guyot determined that to be Newfound Gap, hence the change in the road crossing. The road saw a lot of activity in the Civil War, including improvements by a force made up of many Cherokee Indians and led by Colonel William H. Thomas, a white man raised as a Cherokee who would later become the tribe's chief.

Just 0.3 mile above the divergence of the Chimney Tops and Road Prong Trails, you'll reach Indian Grave Flats, the burial site of a Cherokee guide killed by Union raiders. Just 0.1 mile above that, there's a tricky stream crossing at Standing Rock Ford (you won't miss the standing rock). About 0.5 mile above is Talking Falls.

The trail becomes rougher as it reaches the crest of the ridge and dips over to the Clingmans Dome Road, 2.4 miles from the turnoff to Chimney Tops. For those who want to wander one way down the trail, you can spot a car or arrange a shuttle between the Chimney Tops Trail parking area and the Road Prong Trail at the Indian Gap Parking Area, located 1.2 miles from Newfound Gap on Clingmans Dome Road.

21 Elkmont Self-Guiding Nature Trail

This is one of the best of the nature trails in the park that focuses on the changing Smokies' landscape. The path and accompanying brochure do a good job of pointing out the clues to where human activity has disturbed the forest, and of explaining how nature is responding.

Distance: 1-mile loop

Hiking time: About 45 minutes

Difficulty: Easy

Trail surface: Stable forest trail with a very rooty section at the top of the path

Other trail users: None; no dogs or horses allowed

Best season: Spring for wildflowers, and late summer for profuse mushrooms

Canine compatibility: Dogs not permitted

Fees and permits: Parking tag/fee required if hiking more than 15 minutes (be sure to see Introduction)

Schedule: Nearby Cades Cove Campground is open year-round.

Maps: USGS Gatlinburg; TOPO! North Carolina, South Carolina

Trail contacts: Information about trails, camping, road closures, as well as downloadable maps and a "Smokies Trip Planner" is available online under the "Plan Your Visit" part of the park's excellent website, www.nps.gov/grsm.

Special considerations: For campers in the Elkmont Campground's A through F sites, a side trail leads to the nature trail between sites C11 and C12. Restrooms are located just across from those sites, making them accessible from the nature tail.

Finding the trailhead: Turn onto Little River Road at Sugarlands Visitor Center, and drive 4.9 miles to a left (south) turn toward Elkmont Campground. Bear left (east) past the campground entrance at

6.3 miles, and turn left (east) into the nature trail parking area at 6.7 miles. GPS: N35 39.459' / W83 34.834'

The Hike

The Elkmont Campground area was the site of a major logging operation in the early twentieth century. A logging railroad from Townsend, Tennessee, reached through this area to the heart of the Smokies. The extensive timbering that occurred largely clear-cut the forests, and the trail shows how the wholesale removal of trees has determined where different species have come to dominate in settings that offer them more or less ideal conditions for growth.

The trail leaves the parking area to the right (east). You'll notice what appears to be an old foundation near post #1. Cross a single log bridge with asphalt tread to aid your grip. You can't miss the old logging railroad that the trail follows past posts #2 and #3 before it veers away to the right. A mossy scenic seep appears past posts #4 and #5, where an old spring box sits beside the trail.

At post #6, a side trail wanders left (northwest) of the main trail along the little stream, and then rejoins the formal path as you cross a single log span and start your rise out of the drainage at about 0.2 mile. Notice how the trail rises into a richly aromatic understory of rhododendron and mountain laurel, with galax beneath. At about 0.3 mile the trail crests as it passes a few benches.

A sharp left turn takes you down toward the parking lot. Just above your car, be sure to follow the zigzag of reinforced switchbacks designed to prevent erosion on this side of the parking area.

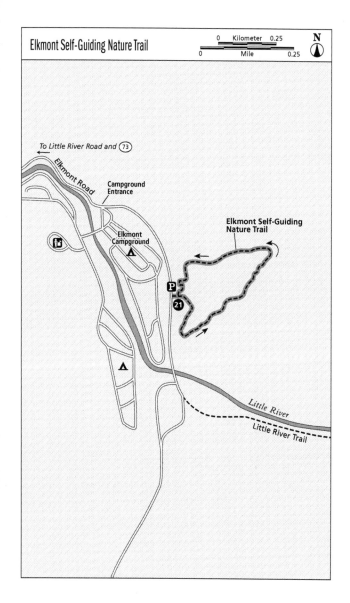

Elkmont Self-Guiding Nature Trail

0   Kilometer   0.25

0   Mile   0.25

N

To Little River Road and (73)

Elkmont Road

Campground Entrance

Elkmont Campground

Elkmont Self-Guiding Nature Trail

P

21

Little River

Little River Trail

Miles and Directions

0.0 Start to the right (east), passing post #1 and crossing a log bridge.

0.2 Rise out of the drainage.

0.3 The pathway is pretty rooty across this high point of the trail.

1.0 Arrive back at the trailhead.

22 Abrams Falls

This dramatic waterfall—the park's biggest by volume of water—leaps off a ledge into a misty plunge pool. Tackle this trail after significant rain and you'll be impressed.

Distance: 5 miles out and back
Hiking time: 3-4 hours
Difficulty: Moderate
Trail surface: Packed earth, but with some rocky, stony sections
Other trail users: None; no dogs or horses allowed
Best season: Spring, after rainfall, and during off-times (such as weekdays) to escape the crowds
Canine compatibility: Dogs not permitted
Fees and permits: Parking tag/fee required if hiking more than 15 minutes (be sure to see Introduction)
Schedule: Cades Cove Loop Road is open sunrise to sunset, 7 days a week, year-round. Between early May and late Sept, it is closed to vehicles Wed for use by pedestrians and bicyclists.
Maps: USGS Calderwood and Cades Cove; TOPO! Tennessee, Kentucky

Trail contacts: Information about trails, camping, road closures, as well as downloadable maps and a "Smokies Trip Planner" is available online under the "Plan Your Visit" part of the park's excellent website, www.nps.gov/grsm. The park recommends calling the Backcountry Information Office as the preferred way to clarify camping regulations and ask trip-planning questions; open 8 a.m. to 5 p.m. daily, (865) 436-1297.
Special considerations: The 11-mile loop of Cades Cove—one of the park's best motor tours—is justifiably popular for its outstanding scenery (a pristine rural valley surrounded by summits) and great interpretation of early Smokies' residents. Pick up the Cades Cove Tour booklet from the roadside information kiosk at the start of the loop. At all but off-times and seasons, or in inclement weather, this can be a

slow crawl of motorists stopping to ogle deer and bears, etc. Do everyone a favor—do not stop in the road for any reason. If you want to look, at least pull off or out of the way so the traffic flow will not be impeded.

Other: If this hike is too much for you, start at the Abrams Falls trailhead, but turn right (north), across the bridge, and make an easy 1-mile out-and-back hike to the Elijah Oliver Place. Notice the "stranger room" added onto the front porch, a feature you'll also see at the Dan Lawson Place farther along the loop.

Finding the trailhead: From the US 321/TN 73 intersection in Townsend, drive 2.3 miles into the park and go right (southwest) onto the Laurel Creek Road at the junction where TN 73 continues left (east) as the Little River Road to (and from) Sugarlands Visitor Center. Measuring from this junction, the campground/picnic area (where restrooms are available at the nearby camp store) and the start of the Cades Cove motor loop are at 7.5 miles. At 5.1 miles from the campground, turn right (west) onto the 0.5-mile access road to the trailhead. GPS: N35 35.467' / W83 51.032'

The Hike

Cross the bridge to start the hike, and the trail wanders streamside on a rocky, stony tread. It then climbs moderately to a crest, and dips into a beautiful dark forest of bigger trees. Now on a packed earth path, you'll dip back down to the stream—the first of three times the route will climb into the quiet well above the rushing sounds of Abrams Creek, and then return.

You'll wander along the level streamside for a significant distance after the first hump, crossing a single-log bridge, with trailside views of the creek. Then you'll rise again, more steeply now, on a packed tread into a drier pine forest past signs of a forest fire (a controlled burn conducted around

2006). At the top, the trail slips through the craggy crest of Arbutus Ridge on a shelf hewn from the rock.

Past the ridge the trail jogs into a really beautiful spot—a sharply benched trail along a rock outcropping with many kinds of wildflowers. Heading down again, the route returns to parallel the stream. Travel a second long flat stretch, where the creek suddenly dances to life over beautiful ledges. A second log bridge crosses a rocky sluice, and you pass through towering, evenly spaced trees in an open forest (more evidence of fire—this one part of a backfire set to combat a blaze started by lightning). Then you'll climb again above the river, weaving in and around ridges into drier woods with more evidence of fire.

At a sign warning against climbing near the falls (and urging parents to carefully control children), Abrams Falls is immediately below but not visible. The trail turns right (north), descends to cross another bridge over a side stream, then follows that stream left (west) to a junction on the bank of Abrams Creek. Abrams Falls Trail continues to the right (north) along the stream, but go left (south), back across the side stream on another bridge to the base of the falls.

The sign at the streamside junction (and another back at the trailhead) warns that a handful of people have drowned in the swirling currents at the base of this thundering cataract (a word to the wise!). A ledge provides safe access along the base of the cliff to the edge of the cascade (but use caution—don't get too close). Never climb on rocks above or below the falls—deaths have occurred here. The Cherokee name for Cades Cove, *Tsiyahi,* means place of the otter. Keep your eyes peeled—you might be lucky and glimpse a river otter. More than 300 were released in the Smokies in 1984 and they often cavort in the pool.

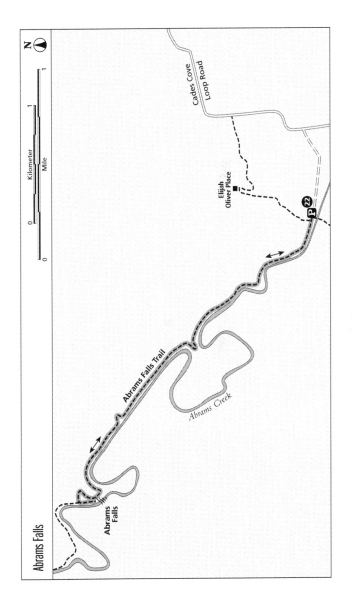

Abrams Falls

N

Kilometer
0   1
0   1
Mile

Cades Cove Loop Road

Elijah
Oliver Place

P 22

Abrams Falls Trail

Abrams Creek

Abrams
Falls

Miles and Directions

0.0 Start from the parking area at the end of the gravel access road.

0.1 Go left across the bridge.

1.0 Cross Arbutus Ridge.

2.1 Pass the waterfall warning sign at the crest of the ridge.

2.4 Go left (south) at the streamside junction and the second warning sign about drownings.

2.5 Reach the base of the falls.

5.0 Arrive back at the trailhead.

About the Author

Randy Johnson is a widely published authority on the Appalachian outdoors. He's the author of the award-winning 2016 *Grandfather Mountain: The History and Guide to an Appalachian Icon*, from the University of North Carolina Press, and best-selling guidebooks *Hiking North Carolina* and *Hiking the Blue Ridge Parkway* (both FalconGuides), among others. His regional snowsports guide *Southern Snow: The New Guide to Winter Sports from Maryland to the Southern Appalachians* won an award from the International Ski History Association. Articles and photos by this award-winning photojournalist have brought the Appalachians to readers of national magazines, newspapers, and major outdoor websites. For decades he was editor of United Airlines' *Hemispheres* magazine, then the country's most award-winning airline magazine. A trail designer and builder, Randy was the founding wilderness manager at Grandfather Mountain and helped ensure the preservation of this significant North Carolina summit as a United Nations–designated International Biosphere Reserve, and now a state park. He was a trail design consultant for the Blue Ridge Parkway's Tanawha Trail and worked to mesh Grandfather Mountain's then-private trails and Park Service paths into the system in place today. He's task force leader for the Grandfather Mountain portion of North Carolina's Mountains-to-Sea Trail and a longtime resident of the North Carolina Mountains. Visit https://randyjohnsonbooks.com to contact Randy and explore his publications.

THE TEN ESSENTIALS OF HIKING

Whether you plan to be gone for a couple of hours or several months, make sure to pack these items. Become familiar with these items and know how to use them.

Find other helpful resources at AmericanHiking.org/hiking-resources.

1. Appropriate Footwear

6. Safety Items (light, fire, and a whistle)

2. Navigation

7. First Aid Kit

3. Water (and a way to purify it)

8. Knife or Multi-Tool

4. Food

9. Sun Protection

5. Rain Gear & Dry-Fast Layers

10. Shelter